Praise for
The Man Who Loved Trees

"A powerful and beautifully illustrated homage to a remarkable pioneer in sustainable urban forest management. Annaliese Bischoff leaves no stone unturned in the life story of Frank A. Waugh, landscape architect and artist."

—Dr. Diana Beresford-Kroeger, Author of *Our Green Heart, To Speak for the Trees, The Global Forest*, and *Arboretum Borealis*

"It is a wonderful addition to any book lover's library."

—Eugenia Bone, Author of *Mycophylia, Microbia* and *Have a Good Trip*

"*The Man Who Loved Trees* is a delightful read! Annaliese Bischoff describes the accomplished life of 'landscape gardener' Frank Waugh—gifted horticulturist, family man, friend, teacher, and artist. It's a rare treat to get a glimpse into such a well-rounded life worth living."

—Julie Moir Messervy, Founder of JMM Design Studio, Author of *The Toronto Music Garden, Contemplative Gardens, The Inward Garden, New Landscape Ideas That Work*, and *Infinite Spaces*

"Annaliese Bischoff has provided a real treasure in *The Man Who Loved Trees*, the story about a most remarkable man and his remarkable portraits of trees. In the early twentieth century, Frank A. Waugh was one of the most prolific writers and advocates for horticulture, landscape design, and conservation of the American landscape, but he is not well known today. He wished for us to see beauty in the common places around us, particularly in trees. Thanks to Annaliese Bischoff, we too can share his deep love of trees captured in this inspiring collection. This book will inspire a new generation!"

—Robert E. Grese, FASLA, FCELA, Professor Emeritus of
Environment and Sustainability, University of Michigan,
Author of *The Native Landscape Reader* and *Jens Jensen:
Maker of Natural Parks and Gardens*

"Rooted in the land, Waugh engaged and taught about landscape joyfully. This well-crafted, highly illustrated book brings Waugh to us through his perception and art to honor trees as one vector in a rich, purposeful life. We all know how important trees are to our planet and all life, so this collection offers us a new window to their value. Thank you, Annaliese Bischoff, for uncovering this delightful legacy."

—Patricia M. O'Donnell, PLA, FASLA, AICP, Fellow US
ICOMOS, Founder and Partner, Heritage Landscapes

"Annaliese Bischoff was destined to write this singular book. In it, Bischoff's impeccable scholarship combines with her background as an artist and a landscape architect who taught a generation of students in the very department that Frank Waugh founded at UMass. Waugh himself would doubtless say she got the story exactly right."

—Mark Resnick, Founder, Resnick Arts and Culture
Consulting, and Author of *The American Image*

"*The Man Who Love Trees* is a fascinating and well-written study on the life and work of botanist and landscape architect Frank Waugh. We were thrilled to learn of his connection to Eastport and the coast of Maine and to a summer art school that existed here in the 1920s and 1930s."

—Hugh French, Director, Tides Institute &
Museum of Art, Eastport, Maine

"Bischoff's discovery of a treasure trove of Frank Waugh's drawings and etchings served as the catalyst for her deep dive into Waugh's life and work. He produced over 200 prints of trees in the waning years of his life. These meticulously detailed renderings illustrate his deep love for trees as living beings, his careful observational skills, and his mastery of the medium of etching. The reproductions of his prints and drawings serve as a visual entry point into Waugh's scholarship and philosophy and a delightful addition to Bischoff's fascinating narrative."

—Liz Chalfin, Founding Director, Zea Mays Printmaking,
Florence, Massachusetts

"*The Man Who Loved* Trees is a compelling story about Frank Waugh, whose many abilities as a researcher, educator, musician, artist, and writer made him an extraordinary individual. I found myself wishing that I had heard several lessons from his teaching before I retired so that I could apply them. The many etchings by Waugh add life and vibrancy to the book."

—Mark Lindhult, FASLA, Professor Emeritus of Landscape
Architecture, UMass Amherst, Co-author of *Digital Land:
Integrating Technology into the Land Planning Process*

"A beautiful tribute to the works and drawings of Frank A. Waugh—a great scholar, artist and lover of trees. Annaliese Bischoff's voice thoughtfully honors and situates Waugh's work for our time."

—Jack Ahern, PhD, FASLA, FCELA, Professor Emeritus of
Landscape Architecture, University of Massachusetts, Amherst,
Author of *Design with Nature on Cape Cod and the Islands*

"*The Man Who Loved Trees* presents the final legacy of pioneering landscape educator and popularizer Frank A. Waugh. Now appearing more than eighty years after his death, this portfolio of etched prints and pen-and-ink drawings amplifies the underlying artistic motive of his versatile and legendary career, which influenced several generations of landscape architects, town planners, and home gardeners in the twentieth century.

"The portfolio is a testament to his lifelong search for beauty in the American landscape and his evolving theory that the finest of places—whether shaped by natural forces, formal design, or incidental land use—emerged from the inherent beauty of trees as representatives of their individual species and ecologically based groupings. This book will engage modern readers with varied interests, including art, printmaking, horticulture, landscape design, regional history, and ecology.

"Prof. Bischoff—whose own career as a landscape architect and training in the fine arts led to the rediscovery of Waugh's prints—provides an insightful, well-researched text and presents a comprehensive gallery of images tracing Waugh's evolution as an artist in the last ten years of his life. Broadening our understanding of Waugh's humanism, the context of his life and time, and the duality of his lifelong love of art and nature, she presents new research drawn from personal diaries, family letters, oral history, and contemporary accounts of Waugh's involvement in local fine arts events. By exploring Waugh's embrace of technical aspects of the etching medium as well as its facility for capturing intricate and expressive detail, she portrays Waugh's images as a visual record based on a lifetime of appreciation, observation and study—both aesthetic and scientific—which had previously enlivened his classroom lectures, field exercises, and myriad professional and popular writings. The exceptional level of refinement and timelessness evident in many of Waugh's prints not only demonstrate his personal artistic achievement but also ensure his enduring influence on American design and culture."

—Linda Flint McClelland, Landscape Historian, Author of
Building the National Parks: Historic Landscape
Design and Construction

The Man Who Loved Trees
by Annaliese Bischoff

© Copyright 2024 Annaliese Bischoff

ISBN 979-8-88824-334-3

Cover Image: Waugh, F. A. (Frank Albert), 1869-1943. Orient Brook: Waugh playing the flute on a rock by a stream, ca. 1925. Frank A. Waugh Papers, Robert S. Cox Special Collections and University Archives Research Center, UMass Amherst Libraries.

Back Image: Waugh, F. A. (Frank Albert), 1869-1943. Man walking in the woods under rays of sunlight, ca. 1920. Frank A. Waugh Papers, Robert S. Cox Special Collections and University Archives Research Center, UMass Amherst Libraries.

Published by

◣ köehlerbooks™

3705 Shore Drive
Virginia Beach, VA 23455
800-435-4811
www.koehlerbooks.com

The Man Who Loved Trees

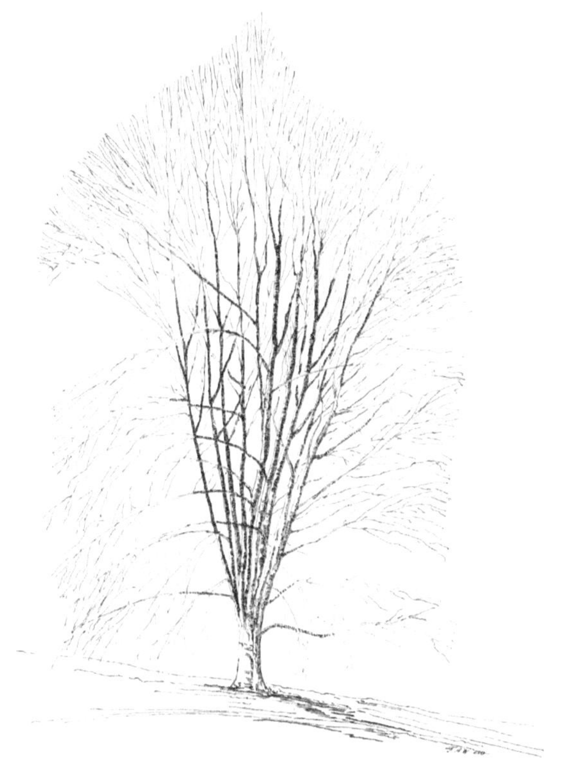

Annaliese Bischoff

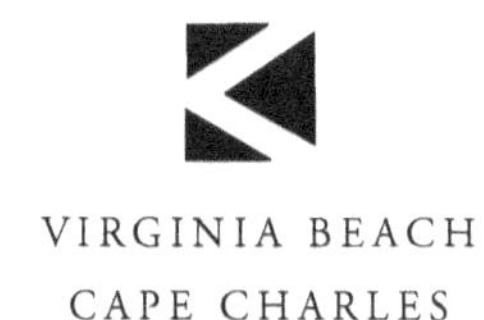

VIRGINIA BEACH
CAPE CHARLES

To C.E.C. Jr.

Table of Contents

Prologue

In July of 2019 the owner of an antiques store in Palmer, Massachusetts emailed me with a question about the value of artwork by Frank A. Waugh. She told me she found a link to a Waugh etching exhibit I had organized in 2003. The store owner explained that she had come into possession of a collection of one hundred or so *block prints*, maybe five or ten years earlier. She found the works so appealing that she wanted to keep some for herself. But she had no idea how much to charge for prints she was willing to sell.

I met the woman at her office where she brought out a tall stack of what turned out to be etchings and ink drawings. Many were in tattered 14" x 18" mounts; hundreds of unmounted etchings were in a large citrus fruit crate amidst miscellaneous papers. Most of the etchings depicted trees, the planting and cultivation of which was the central focus of Waugh's early professional life.

I explained that Waugh was not well known for his etchings, but instead for his pioneering role as an innovative educator and author in the field of landscape architecture. Although he created design plans for some large projects, such as the Village at Grand Canyon in Arizona, and the scenic byway at Mount Hood in Oregon, Waugh is not best remembered for them. I explained to the store owner how I had begun to collect his etchings, admiring them both as artworks and as extensions of Waugh's professional contributions. I had even begun a biography about Waugh years after my 2003 exhibit of his etchings, guided by materials I found at the University of Massachusetts Amherst and The Jones Library also in Amherst.

In addition to studying UMass's collection of Waugh's etchings at Special Collections and University Archives and at the University Museum, I began to purchase Waugh etchings both online and at auction. I also contacted his grandchildren across the country who generously shared photographs and memories as well as Waugh's journals and diaries from 1905 to 1922. What interested me most was Waugh's drive to make etchings at sixty-five, an advanced age in the mid-twentieth century. Why and how had he taken up etching at that age? I thought I was uniquely suited to explore this topic.

Our early careers included time in Manhattan, Kansas; we both had long careers in the same academic department at UMass; we both took sabbaticals in Berlin, Germany; we both learned how to make etchings and pursue art during our retirements.

Sorting through the stacks of materials in Palmer, I identified and purchased more than 150 items. After poring through my new collection back home, I had a particularly thrilling discovery: the citrus box at the Palmer antique store contained a manila folder holding a short prospectus for a book of portraits of trees. Waugh had wanted to do this book using his etchings of trees, but he died before it could be published.

I realized that the focus of the book I had been writing about Waugh had to be his tree etchings and drawings. I wanted people to see this important work. And it seemed fitting to tell selected stories of Waugh's rich life to enhance the appreciation of his tree portraits. This book is not a biography of Waugh, but instead offers background sketches as they led to his last venture. Revealing something of the evolution of his life, these sketches help explain his love of trees.

1

Fruit Trees as a First Love

Frank Waugh loved trees. He planted trees for scientific, aesthetic, and commercial purposes. He used trees in his designs of college campuses, farm woodlots, home gardens, outdoor theaters, public streets, parks, and forests. He experimented with trees and developed many new fruit tree varieties. He wrote more than 300 articles and twenty books about trees. His audience for these works included scholars, arboriculturists, and lay people. He drew and photographed trees. Before retirement, he learned to make tree etchings, hoping to create a major book illustrating their beauty.

The completed book of tree portraits never appeared in print. Waugh's search for a publisher took place during World War II, when paper and worker shortages made it nearly impossible to publish anything. While not intended as a substitute for his book of trees, *The Man Who Loved Trees* showcases some of the etchings and drawings Waugh's book would have contained, and this work also discusses Waugh's etchings and the infectious character of the man who made them.

Frank Albert Waugh (F.A.W., 1869-1943) lived during exciting times. Post-Civil War America, ripe with westward expansion, hosted a transition from an agrarian society to industrialization. Reforms from the US Progressive Era heralded major changes in modernizing education, health, and labor policies. The 1862

Morrill Act enabled the development of the land grant public state institutions, and launched a serious mission to improve the quality of life for common people and communities through practical higher public education.[1] His study at one of these newly formed land grant colleges (Kansas State Agricultural College, KSAC, now Kansas State University, KSU) enabled Waugh to develop his interest, passion, and professional background as a horticulturist, landscape gardener, and landscape architect.

The profession of landscape architecture evolved in parallel with the progressive advocacy for improvement in the health, safety, function, and beauty of communities and countryside. Waugh's career took him to positions in other Land Grant institutions in Oklahoma, Vermont, and Massachusetts, where his sense of vision helped prepare young professionals for service to their communities. Along with his contributions to science, ecology, horticulture, engineering, and public advocacy, Waugh worked to improve the landscape setting of private homes, public open spaces, countryside, and forest land. As his career evolved, he explored his world with the aid of photography, music, drawing, and later etching.

Waugh came by his love of trees naturally. He grew up on his family's 640-acre farm in the open plains of McPherson County, Kansas, and came to share his father's interest in trees. Waugh's daughter Esther describes her dad's background and her grandfather's interest in trees as a hobby:

> "F.A.W. was raised on a large Kansas farm which his father claimed about 1872 as a Civil War veteran . . . His father was a man with an inquiring mind and as a sort of hobby tested many plants in the Kansas soil and climate to learn of their adaptability. He showed special interest in fruit trees and bushes and in ornamental trees."[2]

In 1891, Waugh earned a bachelor's degree in horticulture from

KSAC in Manhattan, Kansas. In 1892 he worked as a professor at the Oklahoma Agricultural and Mechanical College (later Oklahoma State University). In 1894 KSAC awarded him a master's in horticulture and botany. His thesis, "A Preliminary Study of the Grounds of Oklahoma State Agricultural and Mechanical College and Experiment Station, Stillwater, Oklahoma, with a view to their Horticultural Improvement" used evaluations of native Oklahoma plant species, not ornamental or fruit trees, in its recommendations. Waugh published articles about the regional suitability of trees such as cottonwood, black walnut, and Osage orange, further recommending the Norway maple, silver maple, and sycamore for the best street tree in the Midwest.[3] From 1895 to 1902, he served as professor of horticulture and station horticulturist at the University of Vermont in Burlington. During this time, he issued eleven station bulletins, contributed to six station reports, and started the Vermont Horticultural Society on its way. His work investigated indicators of plant growth through studies of physiological constants and enzymic activities. In August of 1898, he received release time to study horticulture under Liberty Hyde Bailey, the country's leading horticulturalist, at Cornell University in Ithaca, New York. Waugh reported that he was "admitted officially to candidacy for the doctor's degree" and was "majoring in a study of plums"[4] but did not complete the doctorate.

Waugh loved his work with Bailey and especially relished the lively exchange, witty banter and good humor of the Lazy Club, the horticultural seminar at Cornell, which included colleagues like Wilhem Miller, noted for his work on native plants. However, as Waugh's own family grew, the responsibility to support them took precedent and would not allow the time needed to continue academic study in residence.

According to family lore, when Waugh decided to withdraw from the program, Bailey made him an illustrated certificate to honor his expertise in plums and plum culture. It was elaborate and witty, a play of words about Waugh's being an honorary doctorate of plums.

This presentation pleased and amused Waugh, as well as his children and later grandchildren. Because no one in the family knows of the whereabouts of this document today, it may no longer exist.[5] Waugh continued with correspondence and some work with both Bailey and Miller. In 1922 Waugh dedicated a *Textbook of Landscape Gardening, Designed Especially for the Use of Non-professional Students* to Bailey as a sign of his deep respect, gratitude, and admiration:

> "For many years I have wished to dedicate a book to you, Writer of Books, Teacher of Teachers, and Believer in the Landscape but never have written anything worthy of such distinction. I have desisted until now, when it appears certain that I never can produce such a book, but yet more certain that my respect and affection for you should find some formal expression. And so for these reasons this book in inscribed with your name and freshened by your touch."[6]

In 1902, Waugh moved to the Massachusetts Agricultural College (MAC, later named Massachusetts State College (MSC), and then the University of Massachusetts Amherst). He headed up the horticultural division and created a program in landscape gardening in 1903, among the earliest programs in this country. In 1907, Waugh described one of his scientific and practical interests:

> "Just at present I am much interested in the statistical methods of studying variation. We are working …on stocks of apple trees propagated on various stocks. I also have some plum leaves sent me by Stewart from trees which I planted in Vt. some years ago … and have Fred Baker at work measuring the crenulations of the margins."[7]

Developing a specialty interest in what had been his father's hobby, Waugh published multiple books about fruit trees. The publisher Orange Judd released one series of books: *Plums and Plum Culture* (1901), *Fruit Harvesting, Storing, Marketing* (1901), *Systematic Pomology* (1903), *Dwarf Fruit Trees* (1908), *The American Apple Orchard* (1908), and *The American Peach Orchard* (1915). These books illustrate both Waugh's scientific and practical approach to understanding and growing trees. The *Dwarf Fruit Trees* volume showed his practical sense of communicating scale, as well as his sense of humor. It included several endearing photographs of Waugh's young children standing by dwarf specimen trees. Orange Judd also published Waugh's first edition of *Landscape Gardening* in 1899. This volume emphasized landscape as a subject of fine art. Whether known as a landscape gardener or a landscape architect, Waugh noted that regardless of the term, "The practitioner of the art is an artist."[8] He would develop this artistic approach to the trees and the landscape later, separately from his scientific approach.

Waugh's scientific approach to trees was appropriate for the time. His *Systematic Pomology* attempted to systematize the study of fruit trees in terms of three subjects— description, nomenclature, and classification. Description was the first step—size, form, color, markings, and other distinguishing characteristics. The next step, nomenclature, the science of names, was very important to Waugh. He wanted the names of different fruit trees to reflect their character, noting that the process of naming can be a difficult, laborious, and uncertain undertaking. [9] As he wrote in his personal journal from 1898 when at Cornell, he expressed his passion for nomenclature in many lively debates at the Lazy Club. Determining a set of standard rules for nomenclature involved priority issues about who first discovered the species and who first published about it. In one diary entry, Waugh revealed some of the struggle behind drafting rules:

> ". . . probably this code will be adopted by the Lazy Club and offered to the horticultural public. Possibly, it will be generally adopted sometime. The only clause which worries me is one

which was originally designed to make it 'incumbent on the author publishing a new variety to use the name given by the originator, or by the introducer, or else to select the oldest discoverable local name.' There is sound justice in such a rule, but it is terribly unscientific, for our aim is to make variety names rest on priority of publication and this rule means nothing but the suspension of the priority rule."[10]

After sorting out proper descriptions and names, Waugh moved on to classification, placing together those varieties with closest resemblances. Of course, this approach seems dated now, in the day of genetic analysis, but it was state-of-the-art at the time.

Waugh's practical approach surfaced in 1908 when he and his fellow Kansan colleague Fred C. Sears bought five farms on Bay Road in South Amherst to establish the Bay Road Fruit Farm with 125 acres for the orchards and more acres of existing woodlands. These orchards contained thousands of trees of different ages, initially mostly Baldwin apples. By adding varieties, Waugh and Sears extended the harvesting season, satisfying the market and making better use of their labor. The varieties they grew included (in order of ripening) Yellow Transparent, Red Astrachan, Oldenberg, Wealthy, McIntosh, Hubbardston, Sutton, Palmer Greening, Wagener, Rhode Island Greening, and Baldwin. They added plums, quince, cherries, grapes, and several varieties of peaches, including Greensboro, Carmen, Champion, Belle of Georgia, and Elberta. The farm included not only fruit trees but also cash and cover crops, often used in experiments to answer practical questions: What fertilizer worked best? Or what about not having fertilizer? What cash crops worked best? Which ones would grow best at different periods than the fruit trees?

Waugh and Sears learned that it didn't matter much which particular fertilizer they used, as long as they used one. On the central plot where they tested the use of no fertilizer, results were measurably worse. But among the plots with different fertilizers, they couldn't see a measurable advantage with any particular one. They found that beans, soybeans, corn, potatoes, cabbage, squash, and strawberries were good candidates for cash crops. And what about cover crops? Which were best at achieving the four main goals—adding humus to the soil, preventing the soil from washing out, checking on the growth of the trees, and adding nitrogen to the soil? Buckwheat, barley, dwarf Essex rape, turnips, soybeans, and rye worked well, they determined. What types of tools worked best for pruning, spraying, picking, and cultivating? They found they preferred a light–draft orchard harrow, the California orchard plow, and the orchard cultivator. They used applications of theory, hard work, common sense, and practical knowledge to build a profitable family fruit farm. Waugh continued as co-owner of the farm until 1927, when he and Sears sold the business to their farmhand, E.R. Critchett.

Waugh wrote many popular magazine articles and books, some under one of several pseudonyms, presumably to protect his professional identity while earning extra money to support his family. Waugh had published under his own name in the highly influential magazine, *Garden and Forest,* until it ceased in 1897. In 1898 he became the horticultural editor of the *Country Gentleman*, a popular publication about agriculture and farming. He wrote articles under his own name on a range of topics for *Woman's Home Companion* and, for garden-based topics, under the assumed pseudonym of Franz Biehler—sometimes in the very same issue. Waugh adopted his mother's German maiden name, Biehler, for one pseudonym. So, it was fitting that he gave himself a German first name, Franz, to fit. In 1915, the Bay Road Fruit Farm became the inspiration for a monthly series written by Waugh under the pseudonym of Robert Lane Wells for his country life "Alderbrook Farm" accounts, also for *Woman's Home Companion* magazine. In this series, Waugh posed as Robert and fictionalized having a wife named Margaret with three children, Robert (junior), Janet and James (Jamie):

"Our home enterprise in the New England Hills. This is the story of a real family who went to farming with the determination to make it pay good dividends, in dollars and cents, in comfort and in happiness. As I am now about to tell you something of our good times and our disappointments, our work and our play, our trading and our visiting, here at Alderbrook Farm, I may properly introduce myself, Robert, age thirty–eight, and Margaret, thirty-five, with the three youngsters, Robert, junior, fourteen; Janet, twelve, and James, seven-just an average American family in all respects, even in our longing to live by ourselves on a farm and have a real home of our own making."[11]

Fictional Robert Wells had grown up on a farm in Ohio (not Kansas) and was an architect by training (not a horticulturalist or landscape gardener). Perhaps posing as an architect showed some of Waugh's own aspirations, or those he had for his real children. The fictional Alderbrook Farm family moved to a farmhouse in the Connecticut hills, not South Amherst. In actuality, the Bay Road Fruit Farm had no residential farmhouse, and Waugh and his wife, Alice, had six children: In 1908 Dan Frank was age fourteen; Dorothy, twelve; Frederick, ten; Esther, eight; Albert six; and Sidney, almost four. Waugh averaged the three youngest children into one single third child, aged seven, for Alderbrook Farm.

Waugh weaved believable accounts of pruning, spraying, and cultivating with family birthday parties, Fourth of July celebrations, and Christmas festivities. He recounted with distinctive family flavor how cash crops fared, the extent of damage to trees by deer, along with general accounting reports. Pumpkins, corn, and potatoes brought good profit. Should he shoot an endearing deer to spare tree damage? Making apple pies from a bumper harvest of Baldwins factored in the fall reports. How could the surrounding forest be best managed? Lumber for building projects? The fictitious Wells's decided it would be very practical to build a chicken house. Margaret kept the books maintaining a wise, logical outlook on what was worth investing. And she took on a chicken enterprise on the farm. An entry about the source of the wood for the chicken house revealed some of the family dynamics:

> "The tangled Alderbrook was both enticing and forbidding. Along its southern bank were a few fine big hemlock trees. It seemed a shame to cut them down, yet they promised to yield a lot of valuable timber. Margaret decided the case. 'Forestry is no sentimental matter,' said she, 'It is plain business. It is not only the growing and conservation of trees, but putting them to good use at the proper time. The old trees must be cut down so that new ones can grow.' Of course she was right; and so it was settled that we would send these big logs to the first good market."[12]

The Waugh family dynamic was not much different, though in the summer of 1908 Waugh took his real family to Wellfleet, Massachusetts, on the Cape, for an extended summer vacation, and not to any new family farm in the hills. While the family continued to enjoy the coastal vacation, Waugh would return to Amherst to run the summer school at MAC and attend the very real new orchard enterprise. He broke away to join his family on the Cape when he was able, to go digging a "mess of clams," fishing, canoeing, gathering driftwood to make an open fire by the shore to cook dinner. The Waughs enjoyed their time by the ocean much in the same way the fictitious Wells's later enjoyed their new life in the country hills.

Although Waugh portrayed The Alderbrook Farm family as being very ordinary, in real life, his family was far from average. Waugh's wife, Alice, was a distinguished, stalwart homemaker and community leader. Frank Waugh recognized this. He authored, under his own name, a *Woman's Home Companion* article, "The Country

Woman's Opportunities," which enumerated social leadership roles for women such as in church work, rural schools, country fairs, and clubs of their own. [13] Alice exemplified such a model role of a country woman in her time. She deserved lots of credit for their children's accomplishments, which began at an early age.

All of Waugh children picked up the sophisticated jargon of horticulture early. One day when Waugh's students were having difficulty identifying a tree in Waugh's yard on the MAC campus, four-year-old Esther distinguished herself by speaking right up. "Why that's a Cercidiphyllum Japonicum." [14] When Waugh wrote his *Woman's Home Companion* article "The Lived in Garden, Make Your Garden a Place to Live In, Not Just to Look At," he included several very competent ink sketches from his oldest teen daughter, Dorothy, along with photographs from the distinguished progressive era leader and noted printer, Horace McFarland, a friend of the family.

The accomplishments of Frank and Alice Waugh's children continued through their lives, as suggested by the following partial list of their honorable successes:

- The oldest son, Dan, lived a remarkable life. His main career was in banking, with several years in Japan, India, England, and then New York. Dan also translated Japanese plays and poems. Working with MAC English Professor Frank Rand they published a book together.[15] Dan also privately printed a book with the help of his sister Dorothy.[16]After Dan's best friend was killed in an automobile accident, Dan took over the care of the family, left in complete crisis. He later married the widow and raised three stepchildren.

- Albert E. Waugh became a professor of economics, later department head and ultimately provost at the University of Connecticut in Storrs.[17] Like his father, he was an avid photographer and authored a book outside his field on sundials. [18]

- Frederick V. Waugh enlisted in 1917 as a teenager for duty in the ambulance service of the French Army and served as part of the legendary Black Cat squadron. Waugh was awarded the French Croix de Guerre for courage and energy. He later enjoyed a distinguished fifty-year career as an agricultural economist with the US Department of Agriculture. Credited for starting what became the Food Stamp Program, Frederick is remembered as an intellectual giant, pioneer, and a leader in the field.[19] He raised three children with his wife.

- Esther worked as a dietician, founded the garden club in Weston, Mass., and raised three children with her husband. As a widow, she worked as an extension agent for Carroll County, Maryland, and then the American Red Cross in New Haven. Carroll County Extension dedicated a memorial garden to her.

- Dorothy (whose artistic accomplishments will be described later) never married or had children of her own. Before graduating from the Chicago Art Institute in 1928, she spent ten years working in the field of landscape architecture for different firms in five states. Between 1933 and 1937 she worked for the National Park Service through the Emergency Conservation Work Program. Her credited projects include a series of travel posters promoting national and state parks. A contemporary exhibit (September 2025-March 2026) at the renowned Poster House in NYC will highlight her National Park Service posters. In 1937 she became the head of the children's book department at Alfred A. Knopf Press, Inc. She also authored and illustrated several children's books of her own. Later in life she authored two books on Emily Dickinson.[20]

- Sidney became one of the Monuments Men helping to save artworks during World War II. [21] He married after the war, but never had children. He designed the 300-pound glass mermaid sculpture "Atlantica" for the 1939 World's Fair to honor the beginning of glass making in America by European immigrants. [22] Among other projects, he also designed the sculpture for the Mellon Memorial Fountain in Washington, DC in 1952.[23] He is best known for his legendary glass designs at Steuben Glass, where he spent most of his career. President Truman selected a Sidney Waugh-designed Steuben glass bowl as a wedding gift for Princess Elizabeth, (later Queen Elizabeth II), in 1947.

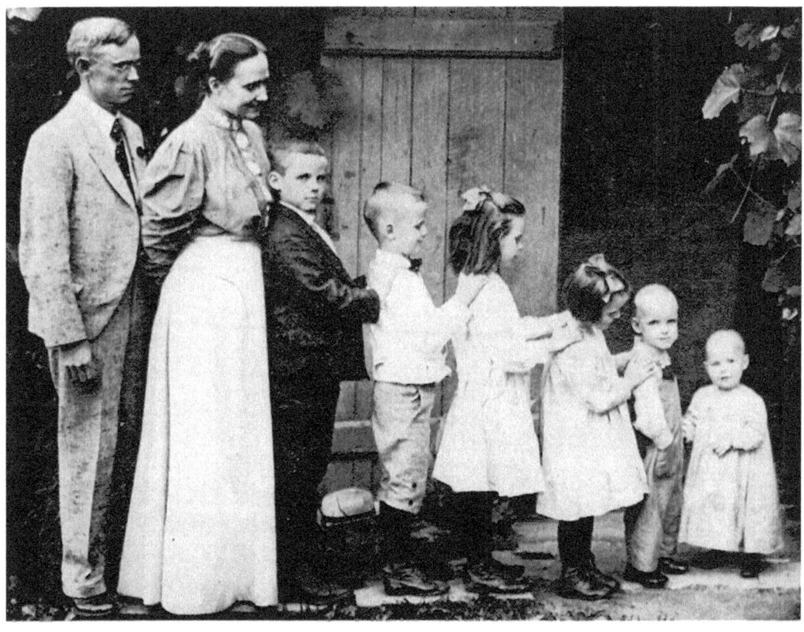

1.1 The whole Waugh family: Frank, Alice, Dan, Fred, Dorothy, Esther, Albert, and Sidney, @1905. With permission from Dr. John S. Waugh.

Frank Waugh was not the only one that recognized the role his wife played in bringing up such a distinguished brood. At her fiftieth graduation reunion, to recognize her success in raising six remarkable children, Kansas State College bestowed unto Alice the honorary degree of master's in family life in 1942. This recognition of his wife pleased Frank. He always cherished his singular family and their accomplishments, as he pursued his own career path.

Waugh's career with its original interest in pomology expanded to cover a wide breadth of landscape architecture, from gardening, design and engineering to country planning, regional planning, and conservation.[24] However, he saw early on that his duties would expand to emphasize developing and administering his college program. At the end of his daily diary for 1907, he reflected on the course of his career:

> "On the whole it has been a good year with a great deal of hard work and more real achievement probably than in any former year. For the first time I have had real opportunities for the development of administrative faculty. The great opportunity came with the summer school, though the organization of the Horticultural Division contributed a good deal and there was some chance, too, in the Grange and in church work. In relinquishing pomology to Professor Sears I took an important step concerning which I still sometimes have doubts. I fear I cannot any more seriously try to be a specialist. I can hardly hope to make a name in landscape gardening to which I am now relegated. It seems to me that only an administrative career is now open - or else stagnation and the end of development."[25]

In 1902, Waugh had been appointed professor of horticulture and landscape gardening within the Division of Horticulture. The Division contained the following departments, each with its own head: floriculture, olericulture, pomology, and forestry. By 1903, Waugh created an undergraduate curriculum of landscape gardening, among the first of three in the country. In 1908, Sears did take over Waugh's beloved specialty of pomology, as Waugh's administrative duties continued to expand. By 1915, MAC developed a graduate curriculum in landscape gardening, a term Waugh preferred to "landscape architecture," viewing that term as favoring wealthy clients over everyday people. Nonetheless, the college adopted the more fashionable name and began granting the master's of landscape architecture (MLA) degree in 1918.[26] In 1931 the institution was renamed Massachusetts State College (MSC), expanding its offerings to face the challenges of the Depression and New Deal. As well as serving as Head of the Division of Horticulture for many years, Waugh served as Head of his department until his retirement from MSC in 1939 with thirty-seven years of service there.

Despite his heavy administrative duties throughout his academic career, Waugh's love of trees remained constant, expressing itself in different ways as time passed. A new poetic and popularizing bent appeared in the 1910's, with his practical and scientific approach to trees moving to the background. The twenties and thirties saw the rekindling of a scientific approach emphasizing the study of native plants in connection to such natural factors as climate, land orientation, slope, soils, water, and drainage. With his humble, practical, investigative nature, he never tired of exploring the world of trees.

Waugh's lifetime contributions to his college, his town, and his profession received significant recognition. In 1941, the Massachusetts Horticultural Society bestowed the George Robert White Medal of Honor to Waugh for his eminent service in horticulture. This award is considered to be the highest horticultural award in America. After his death, colleagues from both his college and town held a weeklong summer Amherst Arts Festival in his honor. Each day was dedicated to a different art that Waugh loved and practiced—music, gardening, crafts, theater, photography, drawing and etching. More details about the August 15-22, 1943, celebrations are available at the Special Collections, The Jones Library, Amherst, Massachusetts. In 1944 MSC President Hugh Potter Baker established the Frank A.

Waugh Arboretum, which has continually evolved up to the present time. The arboretum trees, each with a plaque identifying the species and honoring Waugh, now extend across the entire UMass Amherst campus. Fittingly, the Waugh Arboretum builds upon and extends his legacy. The expanding role the arboretum plays in promoting tree appreciation and awareness of their importance in preserving the climate would have pleased Waugh.

Waugh's late academic and professional career saw the emergence of a new passion— making etchings of trees to exhibit and celebrate their beauty. This passion lasted through the rest of his life and motivated a major effort in his final years—the creation of an ambitious book filled with his etchings and drawings of trees. His hope was that the book would play a role in his lifelong goal of helping people appreciate trees more fully. *The Man Who Loved Trees* presents some of Waugh's efforts to achieve this goal and concludes by describing the role his etchings played in this mission.

2

Waxing Poetic, Reaching a Broader Audience

When Waugh discussed planting design, he advanced ideas to protect native landscapes and enhance the understanding of natural ecology, ideas that were just emerging in the early 1900s. Some of Waugh's views came from his associations with Jens Jensen, a revered pioneer of the American prairie style of landscape architecture, and Willy Lange, a noted German landscape architect.

Jensen was best known for native planting design and conservation advocacy where design ideas followed forms from nature. He wrote *Siftings*,[27] collected memories of his wanderings throughout his life. In 1935 in the style of his native Danish folk school, he founded The Clearing Folk School, a learning center for landscape architecture and regional ecology studies in Ellison Bay, Wisconsin. Waugh and Jensen visited one another over many decades, often in Chicago or Amherst, and exchanged numerous letters, sadly many of which have been lost. In one letter dated March 28, 1938, which survives at the Morton Arboretum Archives, Waugh turned down an invitation from Jensen to teach at The Clearing that summer. Waugh wrote that he would be there in spirit.

Lange was best known for his natural use of plants and evolving theory of *biological aesthetics*, a concept that would later be used during the Nazi era to promote nationalism.[28] Waugh had come to know and admire Lange during a 1910 sabbatical at the Königlichen Gärtnerlehranstalt in Dahlem-Berlin. As Waugh notes in his December 1910 personal diary, Lange sent him the most recent edition of his book, *Gartengestaltung der Neuzeit*.[29] Lange suggested to Waugh that he consider translating his book, but Waugh noted in his diary that it would be "too much for me."[30] Waugh reviewed Lange's later book, *Gartenbilder*, for *Landscape Architecture Quarterly* (*LAQ*) in April of 1923, expressing enthusiasm for not only its content, but also its style:

> "'Gartenbilder,' though not lacking in poetry—even occasional rhapsody—is engaged mainly in an objective statement of the author's methods in garden making."[31]

Waugh further admired Lange's proposal, writing that, "We may develop from the tree cover a complete plant society with all its natural ecological relationships, thus giving a genuine nature motive even to the smallest garden." Associating and grouping plants in line with their natural characters follows what Waugh and Lange called "natural motives," which Waugh further notes as Lange's "hobby."[32]

Waugh believed that the study of the landscape afforded the most accessible, engaging, and effective way for people to experience beauty. While painting, sculpture, and poetry were less available to the average man, woman, and child, Waugh argued that the landscape was available to everybody. When Waugh authored his 1910 book *The Landscape Beautiful,* he wanted to address an audience beyond landscape professionals in the field. With such chapters entitled "On the Relation of Landscape to Life," "On Looking at the Sky," "On the Ownership of Scenery," "On the Beauty of Landscape Psychologically Considered," he was writing as much for the general public as to landscape architects. In fact, Waugh referred to the chapters as a "Program of Essays." The use of the word "program" conjures an analogy of a program of music at a concert. His use of the word "essays" makes the writing more inviting to a wider audience than would the more academic-sounding term "chapter." In the second essay entitled "The Ministry of Trees," he extolls trees for their captivating beauty, symmetry, and life:

> "A single tree is beautiful in itself. Next to the human form the most beautiful unit in nature is a tree. The symmetry of the perfect elm or pine or palm satisfies the eye like the symmetry of a Greek temple. There is something more in the tree, though, than in any piece of statuary or architecture. There is life. And the symmetry of life is always more beautiful than that of any dead or inert thing."[33]

Waugh even ascribed human qualities to trees, thinking of them as people, as he added an anthropomorphic dimension:

> "A tree seems more human than most objects in the world. We more readily ascribe human qualities to it. The oak-tree stands for strength, and the delicate white birch for feminine fragility. The quaking aspen reminds us of the instability of certain men and women, and the somber pine of the cold serenity of others."[34]

He went on to distinguish between beautiful and picturesque:

> "A tree which reaches full, perfect, and normal development is beautiful; one which bears upon it the scars of severe struggle, broken by storms and living against partial defeat, is picturesque."[35]

Noting Liberty Hyde Bailey's two types of interpretation of nature, the scientific and the poetical, which should be kept separate and not mixed,[36] Waugh decided to wax poetic in his book *The Landscape Beautiful.* He quoted from the poets Wordsworth and Emerson, among others. He noted that some artists, especially Corot, have painted trees for their beauty. He also wrote that artists and poets may go beyond their beauty to the symbolism of the divine mysteries, quoting the artist Ruskin's *Elements of Drawing*:

> "As you draw trees more and more in their various states of health and hardship, you will be every day struck by the beauty of the types they present of the truths most essential for mankind to know, and you will see that this vegetation of the earth, which is necessary to our life, first, as purifying the air for us and then as food, and just as necessary to our joy in all places of the earth, — what these trees and leaves, I say, are meant to teach us as we contemplate them, and read or hear their lovely language, written or spoken for us, not in frightful, black letters, nor in dull sentences, but in fair, green, and shadowy shapes of waving woods, and blossomed brightness of odoriferous wit, and sweet whispers of unintrusive wisdom, and playful morality."[37]

To illustrate his book, Waugh selected photographs from albums of the Postal Photography Club, a group of about forty accomplished and serious amateur photography members from the Northeast US. Waugh was himself a member and included some of his own photographs. Interest in his book grew after glowing reviews in such publications as *American Photography,* which called the book "delightful" before going on to recommend it highly:

> "The book will have great interest to photographers and we sincerely commend it to our readers with the promise that its careful study will give them a wider and more sympathetic outlook upon nature."[38]

Waugh continued to refer to his own professional field as *landscape gardening*, in part because he thought it was friendlier and more accessible to the general public than the more professional term *landscape architecture*. His preference was presumably reinforced by the horticultural roots of the nineteenth century term landscape gardening and its appropriateness for agriculturally-focused land grant institutions like the MAC.[39] The term landscape architecture seemed more appropriate for institutions such as Harvard, where architecture—but not agricultural—studies were offered.

Waugh's concerns for everyday people as opposed to those from the privileged class can be seen clearly in *The Landscape Beautiful*. A review of this book in *LAQ* takes issue with his attitude toward the professional field:

> "Professor Waugh says (page 87), 'This chaotic, formative, initiatory state of affairs could hardly be better illustrated than in the fact that the men most deeply engaged in the art have not decided what to call it. . .. One cannot avoid the rather mean suspicion, however, that the present fashion among the professional brethren to call themselves Landscape Architects is promoted by two accidental causes: first, the feeling that architecture sounds bigger than gardening and can command a better fee, and second, the fact that the architectural style of landscape work is the present vogue among wealthy clients.
>
> Professor Waugh's 'mean suspicion' is not so far from a statement of fact. Architecture is bigger than gardening, and properly commands a better fee, and the ground in the immediate vicinity of the houses of wealthy clients, as in the vicinity of any important buildings, often does demand an architectural style of landscape work. Doubtless, a man dealing frequently with architectural elements in his landscape design is therefore the more ready to call himself

a Landscape Architect, but the term is now commonly used to cover the work of the profession in all its branches. The case seems now to be not a matter of argument as to relative merits of different names, but rather a question of fact as to what name is generally accepted. And when the only society of men professionally concerned primarily in such work, containing most of the better-trained practitioners, calls itself the American Society of Landscape Architects, and, when Harvard University offers a professional course in 'Landscape Architecture,' it would seem that 'Landscape Architecture' bade fair to be the recognized name of the profession."[40]

Waugh had resisted membership in the American Society of Landscape Architects (ASLA, founded in 1899) until 1924[41] when he became head of as ASLA committee on landscape extension work. Much earlier Waugh became a member of the American Civic Association (ACA, founded in 1904), as well as a founding member of the American Society for Horticultural Science in 1902-03. The timing of his joining the ASLA dovetails with his increased use of the term "landscape architecture." In 1939 ASLA elected him a Fellow.[42]

Waugh's desire to address the needs of everybody would likely have made him pleased with how the *LAQ*'s review of his 1910 book concluded:

"It would seem that Professor Waugh's book is of more value to the general public than to the professional practitioner, but to the general public it should be distinctly valuable. Lying at the bottom of the discussions throughout the book is the basic idea, which cannot be too often insisted on,—that beauty in landscape is a fundamental need of our intellectual existence, and that the beauty of our common surroundings, obtainable by common means, is a national asset of almost inconceivable value, as yet practically undeveloped."[43]

Not all reviewers of Waugh's book found such value. The author of an unsigned review in *Landscape Architecture Magazine* objected to Waugh's failure to mention Camilo Karl Schneider's *Landschaftliche Gartengestaltung*, a book about design based on native landscape inspiration.[44] The review further criticized Waugh's more popular style and his treatment of spirit:

> "Professor Waugh has a sincere appreciation of scenery, though it is expressed in what are today old-fashioned terms. There is in his writing a hint of the pathetic fallacy shown throughout in his talk of "the spirit of the landscape," but more definitely when he speaks of the tragic sea and mountains . . . spirit to Professor Waugh apparently means the soul of the landscape or the God or portion of God inventing it, but he constantly uses the word as if it were the equivalent of the emotional effect on man."[45]

The review continued with a critical tone, suggesting that his comparisons with other arts, although entertaining, were actually dangerous "since the only similarities to one art and another are in the emotional effect produced."[46] The reviewer found Waugh's suggestion that a park can be likened to an essay and divided into paragraphs to be just plain dangerous, and not even entertaining. The reviewer added another fuss, claiming that Waugh's use of human figures in the landscape photos was excessive and distracting, before concluding with a positive appreciation of Waugh's sincerity to the presentation of the theme.

Despite such professional criticisms, Waugh continued to try to educate the masses about the artistic value of a landscape. As mentioned, he was a prolific author, frequently publishing articles on the value and spirit of a landscape in popular magazines such *Country Gentleman* and *Woman's Home Companion*. A number of his articles appeared in 1930 as a book called *Everybody's Garden,*

The How, the Why and Especially the Wherefore, of the Home Garden, With Emphasis Upon the Interests of the Average American.[47] In addition to being a successful popular author, Waugh was a much-loved college teacher.

3

The Love of Trees and Teaching

Professor Waugh wanted to share his love of trees with everyone. He thought that trees were very much like the people who stood to be enriched by them. Waugh believed trees brought not only beauty, but also truth and joy to people. But it's important to note that Waugh also brought a solid academic foundation to his love of trees.

Waugh distinguished himself as a teacher by combining his passion for beauty found in nature and art with a recognition of the practical value of trees. His Midwestern agricultural background had given him the highest respect for practical, simple farming. This helped him get along well with his predominantly young, male, agricultural students. To some of his students, Massachusetts natives who may not yet have seen much of the world, Waugh's artistic interests may have seemed downright "kooky," as a survey of former students testified.[48] Yet the survey of these same students clearly showed the great admiration and affection they had for their teacher.

Waugh required his students to look, to observe, and to think about elements in the landscape through direct experience of its qualities. He had unconventional ways of getting his students to do so. He would lead his students outside into a storm to feel the changing conditions. He would have them lie on their backs to experience the force of rain drops. He would shepherd them on evening nature hikes under the stars.

Waugh stressed the importance of basic design principles found in nature, as well as in art. Two principles Waugh often stressed included unity and variety. In his *Textbook of Landscape Gardening*, Waugh explains:

> "The first principle of all art is unity. This means that each work of art, large or small, must have one and only one meaning, and that every part shall contribute to this meaning. Stated in physical terms, all parts must be organized into one body, each part being completely subordinate to the interests of the whole."[49]

The second basic principle that Waugh preached in this textbook was variety:

> "Next to unity stands variety as the fundamental necessity in art. Indeed art is sometimes defined as unity in variety. To make a work of art permanently interesting and pleasing a certain amount of variety is needful."[50]

Waugh strived to make these design principles understandable and accessible to his students. In teaching them more about design principles, he turned to music as a vehicle for communicating the concept of a "motif," motive, or theme, his third design principle. In the textbook Waugh wrote:

> "Every worthwhile work of art has a subject, theme or motive. In landscape gardening the term motive is perhaps the most eligible, though all three words mean the same thing."[51]

Waugh used the concept of motive as a means of helping students organize their ideas. He used music to illustrate the analogy of theme. He often played the flute and his pan pipes for his students in class, on nature hikes, or when he invited students for afternoon cookies and hot chocolate at his home directly on the college campus. He also liked playing near a brook in the woods. In his efforts to expose his students to more culture, additionally he would play classical music on his phonograph for them. Tchaikovsky's "Humoresque" was one of his favorite pieces, as the survey by former students attests.

Using the analogy of a classical symphony, Waugh would relate its five movements to five different landscape scenes. He suggested that *allegro* could be like a downhill jaunt through mixed saplings. Next *andante* conjured up images of harmony with tall graceful similar pines. Then *largo* was like a stand of mature specimens, followed by *scherzo*, a stand of competing seedlings. Lastly, the culminating "finale" was an expression and repetition of all the foregoing themes.

Waugh also found an analog to a landscape design's motive in the subject of a painting. Waugh frequently showed his students art prints from his personal collection and took his students to nearby art museums to view paintings. He particularly advocated the landscape paintings of Corot. In *The Landscape Beautiful* (p.316) Waugh advocated having a "well-selected set of Copley prints" or "even a set of Perry pictures costing one cent each will be well worth one or two exercises." Waugh extolled Corot's skill at creating compositions that were "pleasing." He suggested students study Corot's uses of landform and water in his paintings. He guided them to look for general compositional elements and the treatment of the landscape as subject. He then guided students to consider Corot's use of trees: How many trees, how many species, grouped, formal or informal? Waugh would ask his students to describe the design principles they observed in his art print reproductions. He often would pose a series of questions to his students to generate critical thinking. In his "Outline for a Study of Corot's Pictures," Waugh begins with five questions about land and water, three about composition and nine about trees:

"LAND AND WATER
To what extent does he use water in his landscape?
In what forms-ponds, brooks, etc.?
Are his pictures mostly of wild or cultivated land?
What kind of land does he choose to paint-plains, rough
land, mountains, etc.?
Does he show any special preferences with respect to
contour, grade or topography?
GENERAL COMPOSITION AND TREATMENT
Are objects scattered or massed? Criticize in detail.
What of chiaroscuro?
What attention is given to conditions of weather?
To the hour of the day? In how many pictures can the hour
of the day be fairly known without reference to title?
TREES AND THEIR TREATMENT
To what extent are trees used in Corot's landscapes?
To what extent are they grouped?
How are the groups composed? How many trees? How
many species?
Are these groups formal or informal?
How are the groups placed-background, middleground or
foreground?
What species are most frequently used?
Are the specimens chosen formal, natural, or picturesque?
To what extent are shrubs used, and in what manner?
To what extent and in what manner does he use grass,
flowering plants, etc.?"[52]

Waugh firmly believed that outdoor exercises offered the best,
the most vivid, and the most engaging means of teaching students
about forms of beauty and of the natural landscape. He built one
teaching technique on the concept of golf links. He first would
establish a series of station points corresponding to the holes of golf

links, where each station would promote a sense of development, sequence, and climax. In this exercise he called "The Landscape Links," Waugh had his students answer questions at each station in three categories:

> "PARTICULAR VIEWS
> Sketch each view.
> Sketch a ground plan of each view.
> Characterize each view and classify the series.
> Criticize each view and classify the series.
> Each point of view might have been better chosen; criticize.
> Which is the most pleasing view? Why?
> Is the value of any view influenced by extraneous associations?
> THE WHOLE COLLECTION
> Is there any order, sequence, climax or other relation in the series?
> Might any rearrangement, addition or omission improve the series?
> On what principle should this series of views be organized?
> GENERAL QUESTIONS
> Which views are best, -- foreground, middle ground, or distance?
> At what distance do trees give the best effects? Running water? Still water? Lawn? Meadow?
> Would different atmospheric or weather conditions make different answers necessary to any questions on this sheet? For instance?
> Would the course of views be worthwhile in midwinter?"[53]

Waugh required his students to write and sketch both indoors and outdoors. What constituted a pleasing view was a significant question that Waugh routinely asked of his students. The questions

Waugh posed in "The Landscape Links" reveal much about his thinking and provide some understanding of the compositions he subsequently created in his drawings and etchings.

4

On the Art of Grouping

In teaching and writing about planting design, Professor Waugh advanced emerging ideas of protecting the native landscape and understanding the ecology of a site. But he also emphasized how the landscape in general provides people with pleasure. He believed that appreciation afforded the most accessible, engaging, and effective way for people to study forms of beauty. He argued that the landscape was for everybody, while painting, sculpture and poetry were less available to the average man, woman, and child. Waugh proposed that looking at trees one by one could open people up to the beauty of nature:

> "Each kind of tree has its own form and character. The pine tree is beautiful in one way, the oak in another, the palm in a very different form. The love of nature comes to many cultured persons first in the love of trees."[54]

Waugh also viewed the landscape as a canvas on which the landscape gardener could paint, and he discussed various ways to do this painting. One way was to choose the proper size of groups of plants. An excerpt from *The Natural Style in Landscape Gardening* (1917) emphasizes the importance that Waugh placed on the art of grouping trees in design:

"It seems possible to distinguish seven different types of plant groups classified as to form. These are (1) the single specimen, (2) the group of two, (3) the group of three, (4) the larger group of five or more, (5) the row, (6) the mass, (7) the social group."[55]

Waugh goes on at length to describe the importance of the single tree. He notes that a single tree is an abnormality in nature, and is too frequently planted by landscape gardeners:

"The single specimen is, strictly speaking, not a group, of course, but it demands treatment in this same connection. Early landscape gardening dealt largely in specimens. Writers often emphasized the importance of giving each individual room for complete development. Many of the old time gardens were nothing more than collections of individual specimens. This tendency toward specimen planting has not wholly disappeared. In botanic gardens it is appropriate and necessary. But in pure landscape gardening, where the idea of pictorial composition prevails, the specimen method must be curbed. The single fully developed tree, standing by itself, is an abnormality and a rarity in nature. It is, however, a rarity which is very pleasing to the human eye, and the landscape gardener may well introduce this unit with considerably greater frequency than nature does."[56]

In contrast to their overuse of planting single trees, Waugh says that gardeners avoid planting trees in twos. He proclaims this as a prejudice that landscape gardeners should overcome:

"The group of two seems to be habitually avoided by landscape gardeners. Yet I am convinced that this is due to an unfounded prejudice. In many years of sketching and photographing, seeking about for attractive compositions, I have repeatedly been drawn to admire two trees of a species standing faithfully together in the pasture, in the fence row or on the hillside. Indeed I can hardly think of any other unit which has so often attracted my pencil or my camera. Everyone, I suppose, has a somewhat human feeling about trees, as though they possess personalities like our own; and certainly two persons of like character always stand well together. It is the human feeling that 'two is company, three is a crowd.' I am sure that the works of the painters and artist photographers will show that two trees properly related have great pictorial value, and this type of grouping ought to be more frequently used by landscape planters."[57]

Waugh goes on to suggest that landscape gardeners overuse groups of three. He questions why landscape gardeners use trees in groups of three so often, and not in groups of two or four. Waugh advocates for more use of the group of four, which he notes as practically unknown in planting practice. With four there is still room to appreciate the individuality of the trees because that number falls below the threshold to perceive a mass. Waugh goes on to note that a sense of effective mass begins with a group of five. He also notes that odd numbers are comfortable for people to view. He comments that although the row is not common in nature, it has its place in design, especially with straight streets.

Waugh discusses mass plantings, which he defines as "a group of such extent that its limits are not all visible from some chosen point of view"[58] There are two kinds of mass plantings—either pure (of one single species) or mixed (of several species). In discussing mass planting, Waugh explains the importance of understanding patterns in nature. Citing the work of Drs. Engler and Peters from the then-new botanical garden in Berlin-Dahlem, where Waugh spent his first sabbatical from the Massachusetts Agricultural College in 1910, he emphasized the need to understand soil and drainage conditions with mass plantings. He expounded on what a social group of plants is with an emphasis on ecology:

"It is readily observed that very few species of plants exist in nature alone. Thus they form set clubs or societies. And these friendly associations, based upon similarity of tastes and complementary habits of growth, should not be broken up. If we as landscape gardeners desire to preserve the whole aspect of nature, with all its forms intact, we will keep all plants in their proper social groupings."[59]

5

New Work and Play

From the time of World War I through the 1930s, Professor Waugh continued to bring the beauty of nature to the public. In addition, he began serious new scientific research as well as finding new ways to pursue his artistic interests.

On May 24, 1918, Surgeon General William C. Gorgas sent Waugh a telegram offering him a captaincy in the Sanitary Corps of the US Army. He accepted this offer, though in his daily diary he noted his considerable disappointment because the promise had been for a major's commission. Put in charge of occupational therapy, Waugh served two years as captain at the Army General Hospital No. *16* in New Haven. It was natural for Waugh to promote activities outdoors that included gardening and pitching the establishment of health camps in the forests.

From 1917 through the thirties, Waugh consulted for the US Forest Service, and would spend some of his summers traveling all around the country. His work took him Midwest to Oklahoma, Kansas, South and North Dakota, Southwest to Arizona, New Mexico, and Utah, West to California, northwest to Oregon, and Southeast to Alabama, Florida, Louisiana, South Carolina, and Georgia. He visited national forests all across the country to offer recommendations on such topics as roads, campsites, trails, and views. Waugh published a plan for the Village of Grand Canyon, which was still part of the national forest then, and in 1918 a pamphlet called *Landscape Engineering in the National Forests*.[60] A review of his pamphlet in *Landscape Architecture Magazine* praised the discussion as "sane, sensible, and well worded" but concluded with a bit of the usual criticism before closing with Waugh's own words:

> "It may be doubted in the discussion of trail location with reference to the development of scenery whether the treatment of the esthetic grouping and organization of points of interest along a trail is made plainer by the employment of a literary figure - in speaking of the trail as being divided into sections or paragraphs with the culminating view at a 'paragraphic point.' However, as Professor Waugh himself says, 'All this may sound somewhat highbrow, but anyone who notices scenery at all will enjoy the landscape better if it is effectively presented from the most favorable points in a logical series of progressive views all bearing consistently on one theme.'"[61]

In 1930 Waugh participated in a distinguished panel, with Frederick Law Olmsted Jr. and John Merriam of the Carnegie Institution, to advise Congress on recreational planning for the Mount Hood National Forest in Oregon.[62] During the Great Depression, Waugh wrote a comprehensive manual about land use for park and forest recreation at the bequest of Conrad Wirth, a former student who had become an assistant director of the National Park Service heading up the Civilian Conservation Corps. One of the emphatic passages that Waugh wrote in this work focused on the beauty of scenery:

> "The absolute foundation of all inspirational outdoor recreation lies in the beauty of the landscape. This is a statement which may well be considered carefully in all its

points. The fact is often forgotten. Sometimes the beauty of the landscape is sacrificed to other less important matters. More often the mistake is made of entrusting the planning of such outdoor recreational projects to persons who do not have any lively appreciation of landscape beauty, nor any thorough understanding of what it means."[63]

Waugh's work focused on his ideas for public landscapes that always included beauty. His work spanned international dimensions. In 1928, just three years before her death, Marie Luise Gothein invited Waugh to author the addition of a new chapter on North America for the first translation of her classic German 2 volume set[64] into English. Waugh wrote about geographical and physical factors such as soil and climate, before delving into a discussion of native flora in which he addressed trees and shrubs for gardens. Speaking about the index of American plants as very long because of the physical and climatic conditions, Waugh emphasized:

> "There are many notable species of trees well suited to planting for forest and landscape use-dozens of species of pine, fir, hemlock, maple, elm, and oak, not to mention such particularly interesting sorts as the tulip-tree, the live oak, the catalpa, and the magnolia."[65]

Waugh would use all of these types of trees as subjects for his later drawings and etchings.

While much of Waugh's work emphasized practical gardening, it was also beginning to explore more quantitative and scientific approaches. Waugh and his students' field research on the interconnections between water and plants reflected novel ecological concepts. Waugh's methods emphasized careful observation and precise measurement, research innovations in the profession. But beyond that, his earlier poetic style continued to appear in his more scientific writings. Waugh wrote that running water could provide a source for powerful design themes that can inspire the human spirit. He expressed an anthropomorphic attitude toward water, speaking of "singing music" in his 1925 article, "Water Running Down Hill." He further related the form of water to the expression of "the feelings of American life." Waugh described how moving water captures the American exuberant spirit in contrast to the flat water "in a marble basin," better suited to a European taste. [66]

Besides waxing poetic about flowing water, Waugh presented quantitative analyses. In an article "Running Water," he compared the averaged flow profile of ten streams over a five-year period to curves of "compound-interest" or the "biological curve of normal growth" to show their similarity. This paper contained analyses like the following:

> "Further study of stream flow discovers other interesting phenomena. Clearly erosion and deposition must, in the gross, balance each other; but if several stretches of the stream be compared, these two processes have a curiously changing ratio. In the upper (steeper) stretches, erosion exceeds deposition, the net result being a constant wearing away of the terrain. In the lower (flatter) reaches, deposition exceeds erosion, the net result being land building. Somewhere between there must be a critical point where erosion and deposition are equal. Presumably this point will be determined again by (the) rate of fall, which out to be expressible as an angle with the horizontal. These data may be summarily expressed as follows: At the point where the slope is at critical angle S, Erosion = Deposition. Above this point, Erosion>Deposition. Below this point, Erosion<Deposition. These differences, so simply expressed mathematically, lead to remarkable transformations in the physiography of the streams themselves. In the upper reaches, above S, the stream

bed is washed clean, or nearly so. The actual bed is made up of mostly rocks. These rocks tend to be larger and rougher at higher levels, smaller and more smoothly rounded as we approach the critical point S. In the lower reaches, below S, the channel is clogged with the excess of deposited material and the entire valley becomes progressively filled with alluvium. Here the stream meanders back and forth, cutting its banks into the friable deposits, its bed make up chiefly of sand and clay, more or less muddy. The whole character and pictorial character quality of the stream has been changed."[67]

Although Waugh followed a more analytical approach in these studies, his interest ultimately was in character and pictorial quality, as expressed in the final sentence of this excerpt. He used his quantitative analyses and the work of geologists in the service of practical applications for landscape architects:

"Finally, it may be hoped that the man who studies nature thus in intimate detail, achieving a deeper understanding of his landscape environment, will, pari passu, also come to have a deeper sympathy and a stronger love for this native landscape. Perhaps out of this knowledge, sympathy, and love, there may be born in some choice soul the inspiration which will make a truly great landscape architect, capable of masterpieces of landscape art."[68]

Practical applications for the landscape architect between plants and water are framed clearly in the article "Natural Plant Groups" from *Landscape Architecture* from April 1931. Here as Waugh outlined the treatment of the margins of still water with an illustrated cross section diagram, he clarified the succession of the following eight zones beginning with the center of the open water and proceeding toward the land:

- Floating plants-microscopic forms, larger algae, duckweeds, etc.
- Wholly submerged vegetation-pond weeds, etc.
- Floating leaved plants-water lilies, etc.
- Marsh plants-sedges, bulrushes, cattails, etc.
- Marsh meadow-grasses, sedges, many annuals.
- Marsh shrub or swamp shrub-willows, alders, etc.
- Swamp forest-red maple, black ash, elm, etc.
- Climax forest-maple, beech, hemlock, and white pine[69]

To show how trees mark levels of moisture, he presented photographic illustrations of cottonwoods "determining the thrust of spring ice" and gray birches "marking the zone of suitable moisture." Waugh suggested that landscape architects should not overlook the analytic study of water, which is so critical to the study of plants.

In stark contrast to this new serious research work, Waugh organized an informal and light-hearted meeting with eight of his colleagues and friends on November 15, 1921, over supper in Draper Hall, the college dining commons at MAC. The meeting had one purpose, "to talk art." He made a note of this first meeting in his daily diary:

> "The company, however, is chiefly interested in literature. There were Lewis, Patterson, Rand, Prince, Grose (who used to teach English), Orton Clark, Joe Whiting and myself. We discussed drama, etc. and whether we should organize an art club. We decided not to organize for the present, but to meet about once a month and have a good time."[70]

This group would go on to serve as a culture club. It continued to meet monthly for two years beyond Waugh's death in 1943. Initially, the members decided to call themselves "The Intellectuals." They typically met at one of their homes for an evening of entertaining discussions, but sometimes still convened in Draper Hall. The program would typically include supper and one person's presentation on a topic of personal expertise or interest. Topics included a wide range of interests such as Japanese prints, chrysanthemums, photography, landscape paintings, travel, a father's war-time diary, Shakespeare, and etchings. The name of the group later evolved to "Shubenacadies, the Intellectuals." Shubenacadies refers to a Mi'kmaw settlement of Indians in Nova Scotia, where one later member, Fred Sears, did some work. The word "Shubenacadie," meaning an abundance of ground nuts,[71] reflected the sense of playful fun and humor this group grew to enjoy with its meetings. They thought of themselves as "a handful of nuts." The breezy group remained loosely organized, readily allowing for guests and new members, and by 1939 the group included women, mostly the wives of the members.

Many of the members of the group were faculty at MAC. But another later member Ray Stannard Baker, who had moved to Amherst in 1910, was an author who served as President Woodrow Wilson's press secretary in 1918 and would go on to win the 1940 Pulitzer Prize in Autobiography for his eight-volume *Woodrow Wilson: Life and Letters* (1927–1939). He shared his books in progress by reading excerpts to the group. He wrote several letters to Waugh about how much he appreciated sharing his work with the Shubenacadie group. Baker expressed his esteem for the group in a reply to a letter from Waugh:

> "Your note has warmed my heart. I think you know how lonely a writer's life must of necessity be and how he often reaches the point of wondering whether his start on a book or on an article he has written is worth anything at all. It helped me greatly to read some of the chapters of the earlier volume of my autobiography to the Shubenachides. You know the

practice of playwrights in testing a new play by trying it on the dog. Who can doubt the dogginess of the Shubenachides? I found them, the other night, most appreciative and helpful, and now your letter has added to my pleasure."[72]

Baker wrote under the pseudonym of David Grayson, creating an adventure series beloved in its time with such titles as *The Friendly Road*, *Adventures in Contentment*, and *The Countryman's Year*. In his endearing stories, infused with Emersonian idealism, David Grayson's writing captured the hearts of millions. It epitomized the kind of life that he and Waugh actually lived in Amherst. Waugh and Baker valued their country-life time together, especially through the new Shubenachides group Waugh created. Baker kept his real identity hidden from his Grayson name. Honoring this secrecy, when Waugh published an article earlier called "Joys of Fishless Fishing,"[73] he used only the Grayson name as he talked about his fishing companion. Baker remembered that experience vividly as he later shared in a letter to Waugh:

> "Do you remember the article under the Grayson name about our fishing trip up in Goshen? Well, I have always rather liked it and I am going to include it in a new Grayson book which Doubleday is bringing out this fall. I am calling it "Under My Elm." I thought you would have no objections."[74]

The subject of the book in real life was the elm tree on Sunset Avenue in Amherst, on a property across the street from Baker's residence. Baker had become very fond of the view of this tree. So when the neighbor who owned this property wanted to cut it down, Baker became alarmed. He stepped in to purchase the property in order to spare the tree, which still stands today in 2024. This tree became significant to Waugh and Baker's friendship as it served as a subject of a later etching by Waugh, as seen in the gallery chapter of this book. Baker expressed his friendship with Waugh in several notes. To cheer Waugh when he was convalescing from surgery in 1941, Baker wrote:

> "We had notice from Fred Sears of that handful of nuts which you, in your horticultural wisdom, started so many years ago. It is to be next Wednesday, and we shall miss you greatly. But you may be assured that we shall all be thinking of the chief nut of all."[75]

Throughout 1904 Waugh worked with the architect Walter R. B. Willcox, who designed Wilder Hall (the MAC landscape gardening program's new home). He made sure it included a darkroom for his photography and an exhibit space. Beginning in 1905 Waugh displayed his photography in an annual show in Wilder, featuring both his portraits and his landscapes. He started an annual family art show where members of the MAC community could contribute their work. He used the space in Wilder Hall to hang a number of art shows for his students as well as the public. Around the time that the Shubenacadie meetings began, MAC alumni gave funds to construct Memorial Hall as a center for student activities and for alumni offices. Waugh seized the opportunity to organize exhibits in the new space, getting some ideas from his Shubenacadie friends. For instance, the culture club would visit the shows at Memorial Hall as part of their agenda, and Orton Clark, a plant professor at MAC, shared his collection of Japanese prints in 1922. But with the new space available, Waugh began to organize shows from distinguished artists outside the college community, and to book traveling shows such as those provided by the Chicago Society of Etchers and the Associated American Artists of New York. There was also the Postal Photography Club, of which he was a member, where albums of photographs from participating members would circulate through the mail to different cities. He used both Memorial Hall and Wilder Hall for these exhibitions.

In an era before television, the kind of social exchange possible though the Shubenacadie culture club created a structure for amusement and entertainment. More critically, it fostered a creative sharing of interests and ideas, as well as deepening friendship and support. One could easily imagine that it encouraged Waugh's evolving interest in the creation of art, soon to include the making of etchings.

6

Learning How to Make Etchings

In order to learn how to make etchings, in the summer of 1934 Professor Waugh joined other artists at the Eastport Summer School of Art in Maine. The prominent and prolific American artist George Pearse Ennis founded this school in 1922. Ennis, who was born in 1884 in St. Louis, worked in diverse media. He created bold watercolors, oil paintings, murals, and stained glass, as well as etchings. Following his studies at the St. Louis Art Museum and the Holmes Art School in Chicago, Ennis moved to New York City to study under William Merritt Chase at the Chase School of Art. In 1922, together with Walter Leighton Clark, John Singer Sargent, and Edmund Greacen, Ennis established a nonprofit artists cooperative, the Painters and Sculptors Gallery Association, and the Grand Central Art Galleries on the seventh floor of the Grand Central Terminal to feature contemporary exhibits. In 1923, they launched the Grand Central School of Art there, where Ennis taught painting and watercolor during the academic year. By 1928, the Grand Central School of Art chose the Eastport School as its summer headquarters, where about forty students enrolled for instruction with Ennis and fellow artist, Edmund Greacen. Ennis described the vivid sense of place artists would find at this location:

"In selecting Eastport as a prospective ground, we do so with the utmost enthusiasm. It is a region offering every phase of painter-material ranging in scope from secluded bits of shore and inlet to great panorama of sea and land. There are boldest headlands rugged coves, scores of islands- wooded, rocky; there is the odd charm of the lobster fisherman- the picture life of the sardine fleet; there are wharves and sheds and harbor life—a varied waterfront of intensely appealing material, and an old rambling town of interesting streets and homes In possibly no other section of the American coast is the life still so quaint and primitive as in this corner of the sea between Maine and New Brunswick. In the vicinity of Eastport, the question is not 'What to Paint?' It is rather, 'What Not to Paint?'"[76]

Ennis distinguished himself in the arts with numerous awards and commissions. Students felt honored to study with him. In 1929, Ennis had been appointed head of the John and Mable Ringling Art Museum at Sarasota, Florida. In October 1932, he opened the George Pearse Ennis School of Painting in New York City. In 1933, he authored a book about making watercolors. One of the plates in this book features a fishing scene from Eastport, the location of his summer school.[77] Ennis also chose farm and fishing scenes from Eastport as subjects for several of his etchings. Back in 1922, his Eastport program offered only oil painting and watercolor classes in an eight-week program with a tuition of fifty dollars.[78] By 1933, the summer school also offered etching and lithography classes with instruction from Ennis and printmaker Robert C. Craig.

Waugh knew Ennis before he took the Eastport course, but where and when they met is not clear. An article from the Massachusetts Collegian in 1931 stated that Ennis had a summer home in Montague, a small town near Amherst, Massachusetts, and was a personal friend of Waugh.[79] Waugh organized an exhibit of landscape paintings by Ennis (valued even then at over $50,000, according to a *Massachusetts*

Collegian news article from November 18, 1931) in the lounge of the Memorial Hall at the Massachusetts Agricultural College (MAC) in 1931. An earlier article from 1930 reported that Waugh secured about thirty Ennis landscape paintings from the Grand Central School of Art for an exhibit in Memorial Hall in January that year. That article noted, "Mr. Ennis spends his summers in Montague and does much of his painting in Provincetown, the scene of many of the pictures of the exhibit."[80] Waugh had summered in Provincetown with his family a few times and occasionally lectured in Montague. It is uncertain whether Waugh and Ennis first met in Amherst, Provincetown, Montague, or New York.

Waugh joined the program in Eastport with fifteen other pupils under the tutelage of both Ennis and Craig. On the first day June 25, he joined the group for outdoor life drawing exercises. On June 28, 1934, as the sole student of Craig, Waugh created his own first etching. His elected subject matter depicted the local character near Eastport, which Ennis had so enthusiastically described. His "Low Tide at Lubec" 5x4" etching features the wharves in Lubec, a town near Eastport. Waugh's subject features the tall timber pilings supporting the wharves—not a portrait of live trees, but trees employed in a practical application.

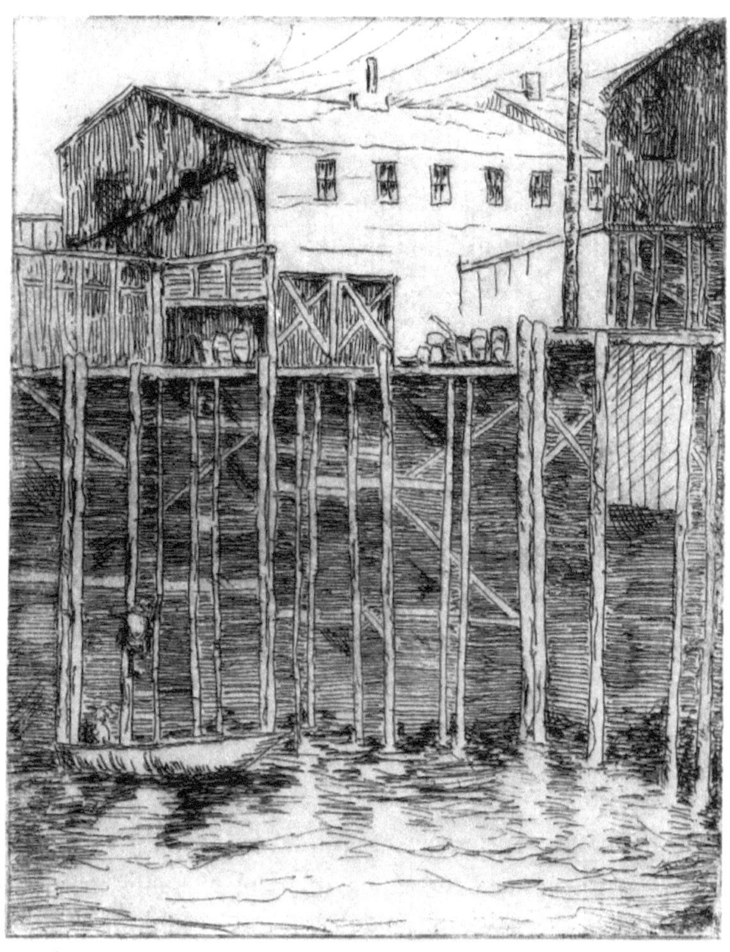

6.1 Waugh Etching, Low Tide at Lubec, 5x4, 1934 (The alignment on the sheet
of this impression of a first printing is not quite straight. Even so, Waugh was
pleased with the result.)

In order to make an etching, Waugh learned the technique of
intaglio, from the Latin *to incise* or *carve.* Printmaker Levon West
explained the process in his classic book, first in the "How to Do
It Series," which later featured a book on watercolors by Ennis. To
prepare a metal plate, copper or zinc, Waugh would file down the

narrow edges of the plate's perimeter at a forty-five-degree angle. Before incising lines into the plate, he would roll or paint a waxy medium, an acid-resistant, brown-colored substance known as *asphaltum,* onto a cleaned and warmed plate, a method known as *hardground.* After that coated surface cooled and dried, Waugh would draw lines onto the plate using a scribe or needle, which would remove the asphaltum. When the drawing was far enough along, Waugh would place the plate in an acid bath—ferric chloride and water for copper plates, nitric acid and water for zinc. The acid would bite into the revealed lines, making even grooves.

To prepare the bitten plate for a print, or a proof, Waugh would remove the asphaltum with a solvent like turpentine. Next, he would ink the entire cleaned plate with an etching, typically pigment mixed with a linseed burnt plate oil, and warm the plate to make sure the ink seeped evenly into all the grooves. Then, he would wipe the ink off the surface of the plate in rhythmic even, circular motions, using a mounded bit of cheesecloth, or muslin. When the surface of the plate was clean, with the ink remaining only down in the bitten grooves, he would wipe the filed edges of the plate clean. He would soak the paper for printing in a bath and then drain the excess water. Waugh would next place the wiped, inked plate facing upward on a large protective dry sheet of paper on the horizontal movable bed of a high-pressure, hand-cranked press. The base sheet of paper can help register and align the plate, as well as keep the bed of the press clean. Waugh would also line up the moist paper so that the print would drop correctly on top of the wiped, inked plate resting on the dry base sheet of paper. If Waugh set the paper down askew to the plate, the impression on the print would be crooked.

At this stage, there is a base sheet of dry paper resting on the bed of the press with an inked metal plate aligned on top, and the moist sheet of paper covering the plate, making a mechanical sandwich. Most of the bed would sit ahead of a heavy metal cylindrical drum. Waugh would then take one end of a thick felt or wool blanket (or two) to tuck under the drum of the press before bringing the other end of the blanket forward to fall upon and cover the moist paper-plate sandwich. Then he would be ready to turn the crank of the press to advance the bed forward so the paper and plate passes under the pressure of the drum, squeezing out the ink trapped in the grooves onto the receptive paper. Waugh would advance the bed, which held the blanket, moist paper, and metal plate, forward under the drum and continuing to the other side of the drum. Finally, Waugh would lift the felt blanket, roll it back over the drum, and then begin pulling the damp print away from the plate to hang (it) up to dry. An example of a finished print "being pulled" from the plate on a press shows a typical setup.[81] Here the felt blankets, rolled up over the drum after printing, are visible. After pulling the print, Waugh would then clean the plate of residual ink to make more prints.

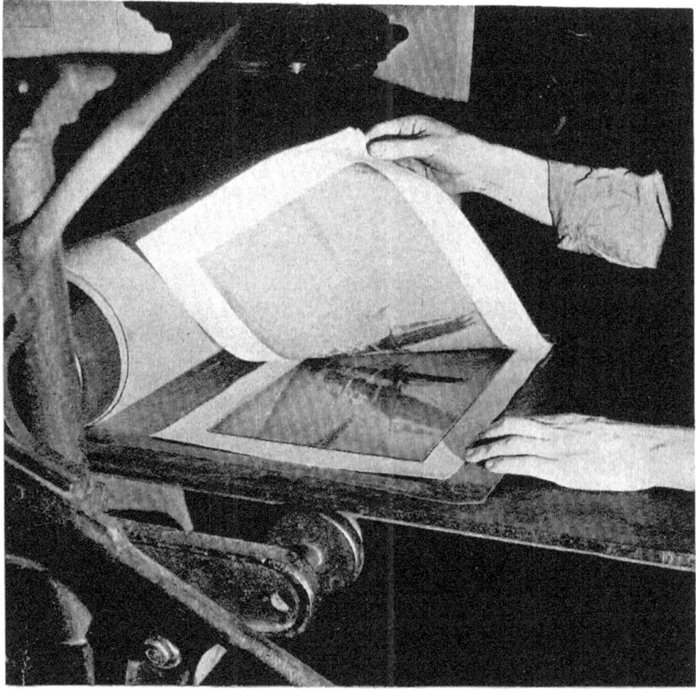

6.2 A Pulled Print, from Levon West's Making an Etching, 1932

If Waugh liked the proof or the state of the print, he could make more prints from the plate. And for each new print, he would repeat the inking process. If Waugh desired any changes and additional lines, he would paint more hard ground to protect existing lines from further biting, and then incise new lines, ready for another acid bath. He would even burnish some old lines out to remove them. The process was tedious, but exciting, too.

The second print that Waugh created in Eastport used the technique of *drypoint* on a zinc plate and called it, "Farm Buildings-Eastport," 4x5". Another form of intaglio, drypoint utilizes a more direct process than the hardground etching process. Here, Waugh used a scribe or needle to scratch lines directly into the surface of the metal plate. When Waugh was ready to see what his gouged-out lines would look like, he would follow the same process for inking and wiping the plate and preparing the paper. In his Eastport drypoint, however, the lines that make up a scene of local farmhouses are different from those in the first etching. The drypoint lines printed softer and blurrier than those earlier crisper lines, so evenly bitten down by acid. The scribe created drypoint lines on a metal plate that were like a plow making an uneven furrow in a field of dirt. The dirt displaced by the plow was like the metal dislodged from the scratched grooves of the lines. Imagine how ink in the wiping process from such a plate would more easily remain trapped along the edges of the grooves, thus creating a blurrier result in the final print.

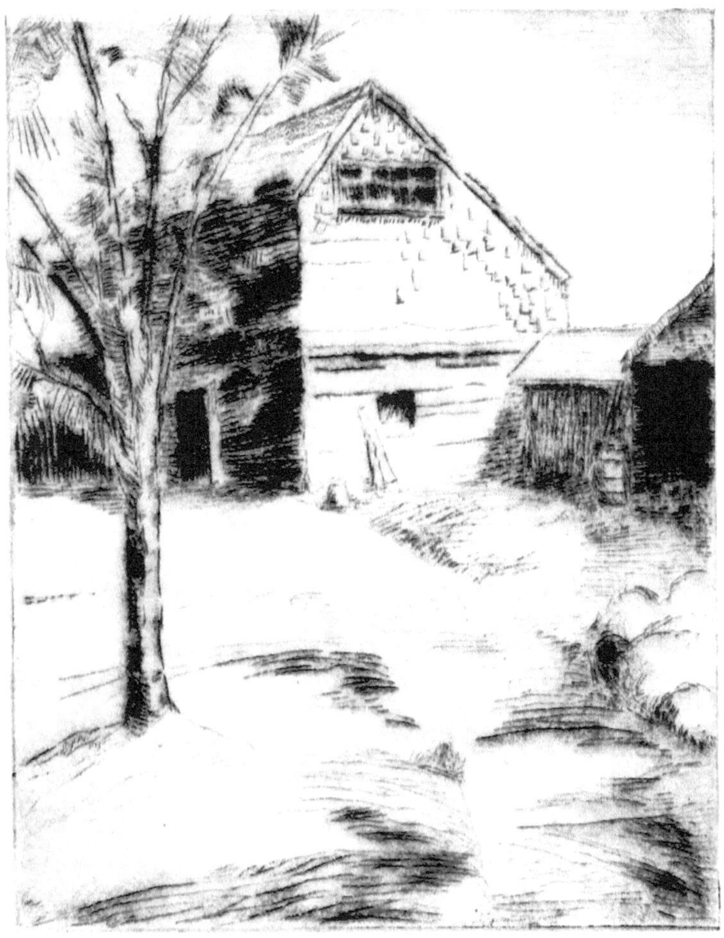

6.3 Waugh Drypoint, Farm Buildings- Eastport, 5x4, 1934

In his sixth etching, "Sardine Factories - Eastport," 6x8", Waugh captured the sense of place well. His view is much like the ones favored in Eastport postcards, still available today in vintage collections. Most all of the lines in his etching are hard and crisp. Yet, a few of the lines reveal a bit of softness. Sometimes artists combine both hardground and drypoint etching techniques on one plate—a bit of a hybrid method. It is possible that Waugh incised a few additional lines selectively in this plate with a scribe, in a drypoint fashion, after biting it in an acid bath. However, he does not indicate the use of drypoint in his list for this print.[82] How many proofs and how many final prints Waugh printed of any etching is unknown. Some artists track the number of prints in a final edition by writing down the number of the print and the size of the edition, such as 1/30, which would indicate the first print out of a limited edition of thirty. However, Waugh never kept track of his prints this way. Moreover, he did not note the size of his prints. Some artists believe that a plate for etching and drypoint can only yield about thirty prints, while others may imagine as many as 100.[83]

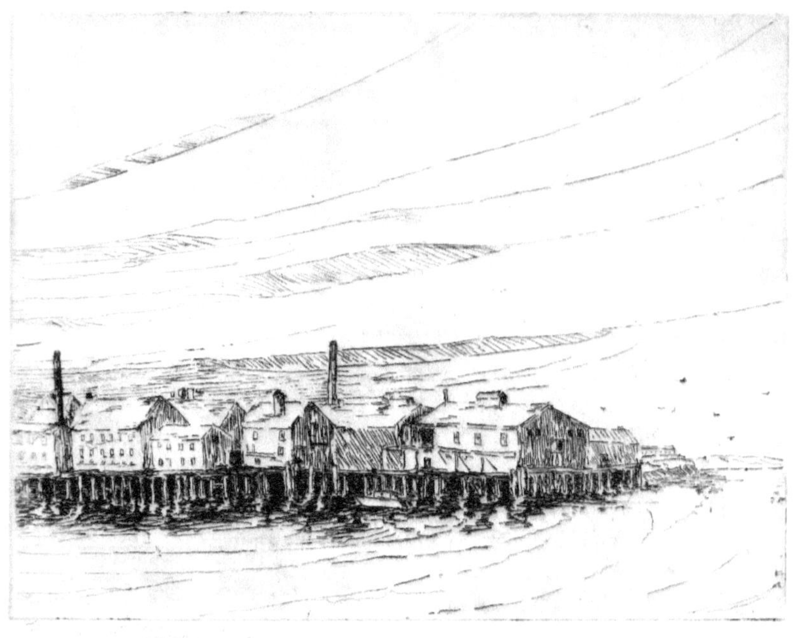

6.4 Waugh Etching, Sardine Factories, Eastport, 6x8, 1934

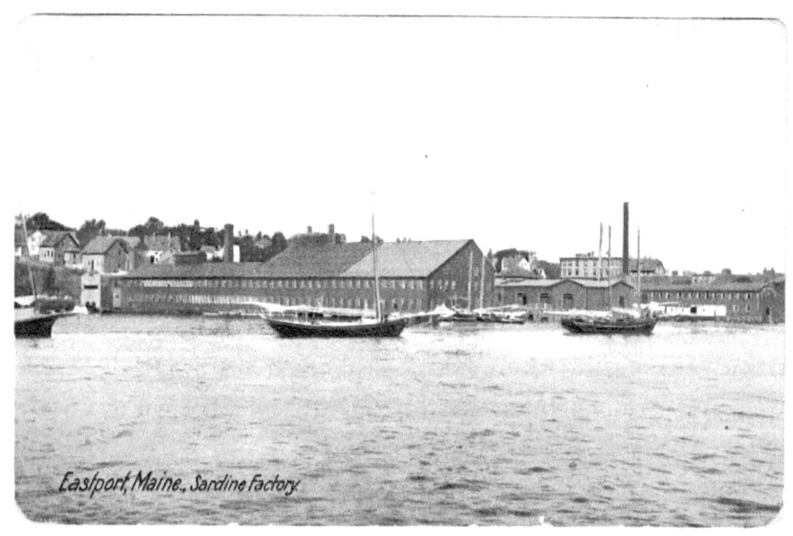

6.5 Post Card of Sardine Factories in Eastport

During the summer of 1934, Waugh became proficient with both hardground etching and drypoint. Later in 1934, Waugh purchased equipment for etching, which he used in his home at the MAC campus, all but a printing press.[84] He had tried to use an available letter press but learned that did not work out for printing etchings. By January of 1935, Waugh's younger colleague and fellow artist Stephen Hamilton set up an etching press that Waugh was welcome to use in the old plant building. Additionally, Waugh sometimes sent off plates to be printed at a shop in Cambridge. Waugh created fifteen additional etchings and drypoints without any note of month. In 1936, Waugh listed ten etchings, again without months. Beginning with the month of April 1936, he noted the months of all his subsequent etchings and drypoints on his lists. Waugh divided his etchings into series of fifty. The list of completed etchings "First Series" includes works 1-50, from 1934 through part of September of 1936. The "Second Series" begins in September 1936 with 51, "Pollard Oaks, Epping Forest", and continues through 100, "Old Plum Trees, Nara, Japan" May 1938. Many of his early etchings featured old mills, but trees become prominent by the second series. The Appendix of this book offers the complete list as Waugh compiled it, and additional notations of which etchings are in public collections today.

Waugh remained in touch with both Ennis and Craig after 1934. The *MAC Collegian* reported that Waugh organized an exhibit of Ennis watercolors and Craig lithographs in December of 1935 in Memorial Hall at MAC, writing, "The display has been secured by Prof. Waugh, who has studied under both artists in Eastport, Maine."[85] Tragically, Ennis died in a car crash in Utica, New York, in August of 1936 when he was only age fifty-two. Waugh lost both a friend and teacher.

7

On Becoming an Artist

In the summer of 1937, Professor Waugh decided to polish his etching skills by spending two months at the prestigious School of Fine Arts in Fontainebleau, France. Understanding his choice of this venue provides insight into his relationships with his talented offspring, as well as into his own attitude toward art.

His youngest son, Sidney, who began college study at the Massachusetts Institute of Technology (MIT) in Cambridge in the 1920s, went to Fontainebleau in 1926 to continue his studies. At MIT, Sidney had wanted to study sculpture, but his father had overruled him, insisting that his son study something practical, something that would help him earn a good living. Waugh did not believe that his son could earn a decent wage as an artist. So Sidney began to follow the full program of studies in architecture at MIT, as his father had so strongly advised. But Sidney also doubled up his studies to study sculpture, his true passion, as well. Unfortunately, with this self-imposed double workload, Sidney became so ill that in 1923 he had to leave MIT to return home to his family in Amherst. He briefly took courses at Amherst College, but never read any program for a degree there, nor did he finish his degree at MIT.

By this time, Frank Waugh had successfully made a name for himself in landscape architecture, a feat he had feared as a younger man would be very difficult to accomplish. In 1922 Waugh published his *Textbook of Landscape Gardening, Designed Especially for the Use of the Non-professional Student*.[86] In 1926 a third expanded edition of *Book of Landscape Gardening* was published. In 1927 Waugh scored a major coup when Mary Luise Gothein was translating her acclaimed *History of Garden Art* into English. She invited Waugh to write a chapter on North American landscape architecture. Along the way to his fame Waugh had been happy to invite his children Dorothy and Sidney to contribute their illustrations to some of his books and articles. Those credits included Sidney's design and drawing "Pool with Principal Terminus" in Waugh's 1927 book *Formal Design in Landscape Architecture*.

Meanwhile Sidney convinced his family to support his art studies in Europe first in Rome, at the Scuola delle Belle Arte, next in Paris, and then at the School of Fine Arts in Fontainebleau. He studied under the renowned sculptors Emile Bourdelle, Henri Bouchard, and Louis Lejeune. Sidney revealed his father's fondness for Germany when he wrote in a letter, "I am just as anxious to study in Germany as you are to have me, as yet I have located nothing and perhaps will not be able to . . .. The best known summer school of art in Europe is at Fontainebleau."[87]

The Fontainebleau summer school program had been established in 1923, apparently partly in response to dwindling interest among American students to spend years of study at the École des Beaux Arts in Paris. The Fontainebleau school offered courses in etching, architecture, still life and landscape painting, and interior design, as well as sculpture.

Sidney spent three intensive months, from the end of June through the end of September 1926, at the School of Fine Arts in Fontainebleau. He stayed in Fontainebleau for two additional years following the formal summer program. He sent periodic reports back to his family about his progress, usually with apologies for not writing more often.

Letters to his family reveal how Sidney had to account for every penny of their support, for instance justifying the expense for a second pair of shoes by arguing that the work of a sculptor required spending so much time on his feet that a second pair of shoes was essential for relief. Sidney Waugh successfully entered his sculptures into exhibitions and was awarded medals at the Paris Salon de Printemps in 1928 (a bronze medal) and 1929 (a silver medal). In 1929, Sidney won the Prix de Rome in sculpture from the Rinehart School of Sculpture in Baltimore to return to Italy for an additional three years of study as a fellow at the American Academy in Rome. He returned to the States with outstanding credentials. He established himself as an associate with Steuben Glass in New York, becoming chief associate designer in 1935. In *Writing for the Metropolitan Museum of Art Bulletin* in October of 1936, art historian H. E. Winlock concluded his article "The History of Glass: An Exhibition" with an illustration of a vase by Sidney, which he presented as an example of the virtues of the Renaissance in glass cutting and engraving (v. 31, No. 10, p. 197). [88] In 1939, Sidney was honored with an honorary master's degree from Amherst College; he later created the pediment sculpture of Apollo for the Mead Art Museum there.

Sidney was not the only one of Professor Waugh's children with a successful career in the arts. Dorothy worked for nurseries and landscape architecture firms in several states before focusing on a career in graphic art. She graduated from the Art Institute of Chicago in 1928 and became a successful children's book author and illustrator.

By 1931 Dorothy's first book came out, *Among the Leaves and Grasses*.[89] From Rome, Sidney wrote his congratulations in a letter to his sister after he received a copy. He wrote that he "devoured it" and ". . . not only liked it immensely, but learned a lot about insects."[90] Next, Dorothy became a noted poster designer with the National Parks Service (1933-1937) through the Emergency Conservation Work Act of 1933. In 1937 Dorothy went on to head the children's book department at Alfred A. Knopf.

Despite the Great Depression, where one might think it would be impossibly challenging to make a living in the arts, Waugh watched two of his children forge notable careers in the art world, despite his own earlier misgivings about Sidney's career path.

One has to assume that Professor Waugh's choice of Fontainebleau to continue his etching studies was influenced by Sidney's experience there. With the sudden tragic death of George Pearse Ennis in 1936, Professor Waugh lost a revered teacher. He needed to find a new place to study.

The best accounts of Waugh's studies in Fontainebleau from the summer of 1937 come from his diary entries. Several of his etchings have titles or description that indicate their creation on the grounds of Fontainebleau. The first, "No. 76 Les Pins, Fontainebleau" features two pines with nominal space between them and a simple backdrop with little perspective.

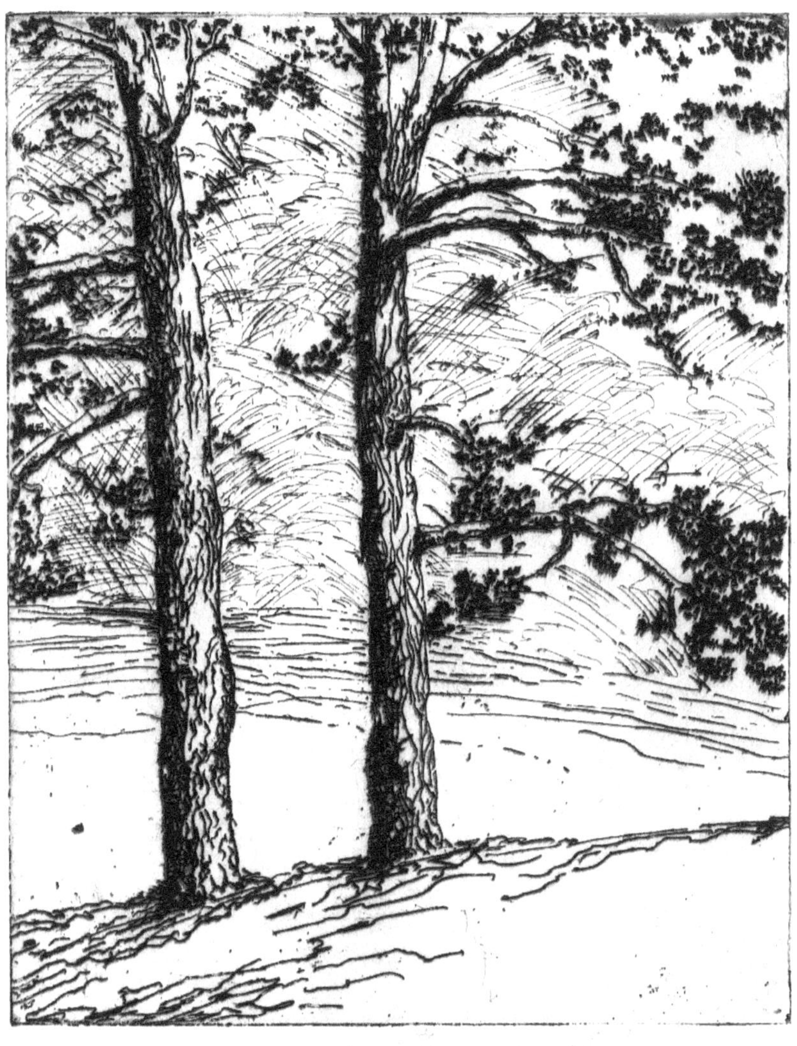

7.1 Les Pins, Fontainebleau, 5x4, July 1937

Another in "No. 77 Les Hêtres, Forêt de Fontainebleau", two beeches standing closer together, as if spooning, are offset by a sapling midground with a more distinct forested background.

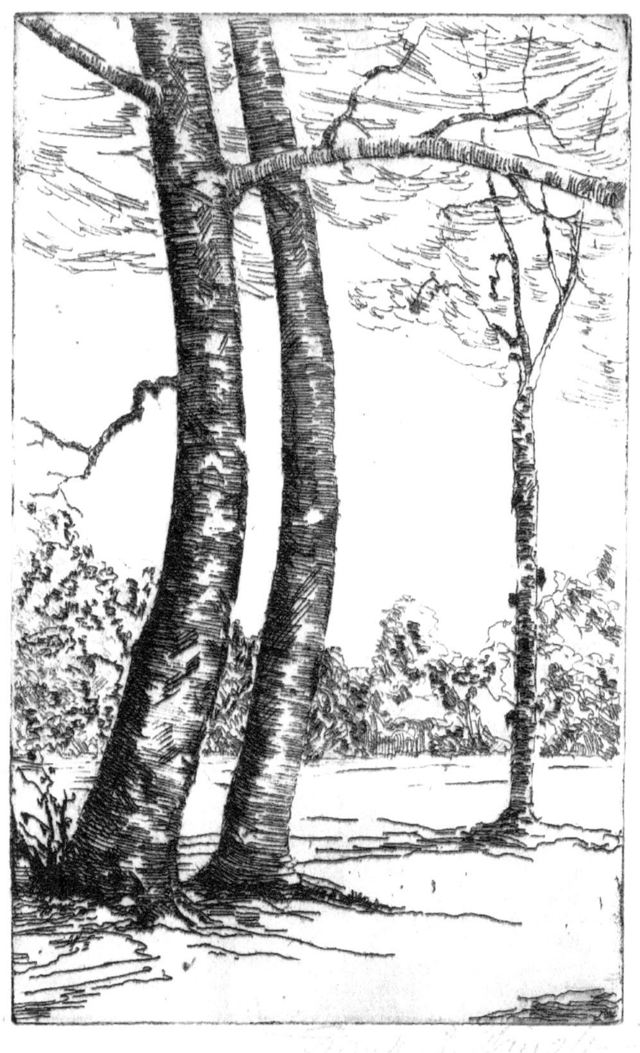

7.2 Les Hêtres, Forêt de Fontainebleau, 6x4, July 1937

"No. 80 Lac aux Carps, Fontainebleau", an evenly spaced trio of stately trees, elms, form the subject with the palace itself in a faded background perspective. In this etching a masterful use of value helps define the composition; Waugh's diary notes indicate his pride in this one.

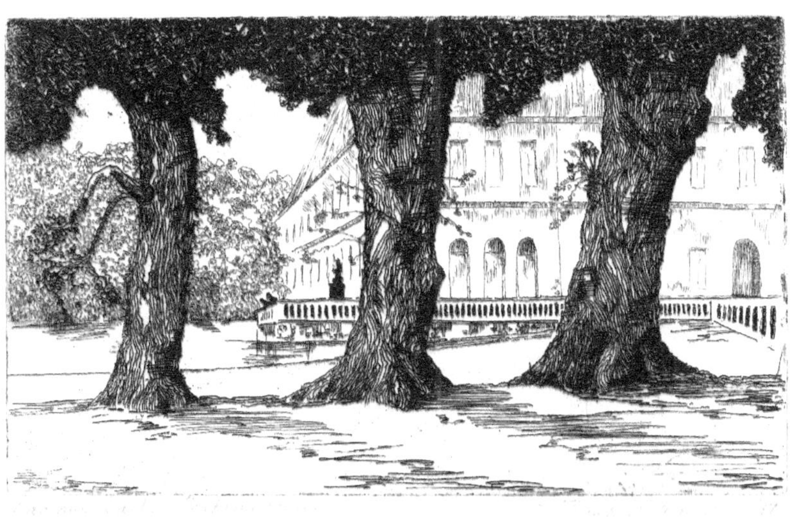

7.3 Lac aux Carps, Fontainebleau, 4.5x7.5, August 1937

The use of value to emphasize a sense of space with a clear perspective view is evident in his Fontainebleau etchings. Waugh learned how to use simple horizontal lines in drawing on the plate to simulate distance and a sense of perspective. By creating lines that were closer together in the background, the distance looked farther away. By contrast, the foreground was made to look closer by leaving more space between lines. The use of diagonals in the composition contributed to a one-point perspective view. And Waugh further learned to create heavier, darker lines to emphasize focal points in the foreground by etching more delicate, lighter lines in the background.

Later in the course, Waugh's etching instructor Achille Ouvré gave two demonstrations of the aquatint process of etching, which typically used a powdered resin melted onto a plate to give granular, tonal effects. In his diary entries during the week of August 13, 1937, Waugh noted that Ouvré used sandpaper with one demonstration rather than the traditional resin. Coarse sheets or patches of sandpaper were placed face down upon a plate coated with hardground, which together were run through an etching press. The sand grains poked into the hardground leaving a pebbled surface. The plate was next submerged into an acid bath for biting. Rich tonal values created with this method contrasted with the values achieved using a linear approach. Waugh was unsuccessful with all his aquatint experiments while in Fontainebleau, which he reported in his diary. But he was very determined to try more aquatint experiments back at home, where it would take him a few years to master, details of which are spare. Waugh was clearly devoting more thought to the development of tonal values during this time.

One interesting side note is that the year after his return from Fontainebleau, Waugh gave Sidney a copy of his *Hardy Shrubs* book, which had been published back in 1928, when Sidney was still in Fontainebleau. It contained the following inscription: "To my famous offspring from a near famous Dad, F.A.W., July 2, 1938." Waugh drew a sketch of a house between two shade trees to the left of this inscription. Was there a particular occasion for this gift? In 1938 Sidney's first book, *The Art of Glass Making,* came out.[91] Waugh's inscription in his own book to Sidney documents how proud he was of his son.

Waugh's interest in creating etchings had begun in 1934, in anticipation of retirement. Although he had earlier chosen a practical and dependable path that allowed him to support his family, did he ever rue a career in art that was not to be? Was the interest in focusing on art in the last eight years of his life a way to compensate for the road not taken earlier, or just a new opportunity that was now opening? Had his two children shown him that a career in art was in fact quite doable? And was Waugh satisfied enough with his near-famous status as he had put it in his book inscription? In 1941 on the occasion commemorating his KAC 1891 class graduation, Waugh edited a publication, "Fifty Years After." He compiled letters from his classmates. In his own letter, he thoughtfully summarized his life to date. Because the letter provides such a useful context, it appears below in its entirety.

Dear Classmates:

I was married in 1893 to Alice Vail '92. This was the most important event in my biography. We have six children, enumerated with their children, as follows:

(1) Dan F., b. 1894, banker in Wall St., many years in Japan. Has three stepchildren, Amos, Enid, and Joan. (2) Dorothy, b. 1896, artist and editor, New York City. (3) Frederick V., b. 1898, economist with U.S. Dept. of Agriculture, has three children, Margaret, Prudence and Douglas. Ph.D. Columbia and Croix de Guerre from World War I. (4) Ester, b. 1900, housewife, Weston, Mass., m. Nathan W. Gillette, 1922, three children, Lois, Mavis and Alfred. (5) Albert E., b. 1902, professor of economics, University of Connecticut; has two children, John and Robert. (6) Sidney, b. 1904, sculptor, New York City.

I have spent my life as a college professor in Oklahoma, Vermont and Massachusetts. Received two honorary degrees, D.Sc. from our Alma Mater and L.H.D. from University of Vermont. Served as Captain in World War I. I have lived (outside of hotels) for a few months in Germany, England France and Japan; I worked several summers for the US Forest Service and have visited every state in the union and all provinces in Canada. In 1939 I was forcibly retired (state law) from my college teaching. My present hobby and chief occupation is art, specifically etching.

Alice and I remain on the college campus in the house we have occupied for 39 years and where we are beginning to feel at home. We are very proud of all our children and grandchildren; I am also still proud as ever of the Class of '91 and of our illustrious classmates; including those who like Phil Creager, John Morse, Ben Skinner, Sam Van Blarcom, Cal Stingley, Nellie McDonale, Gertie Coburn and the others, have graduated to the higher degree.

Ever yours,

Frank A. Waugh[92]

8

Learning to See

After Professor Waugh turned seventy in July of 1939, he prepared to leave for Ogunquit, Maine. He wrote to his daughter Dorothy, "I am getting cleaned up and prepared to leave tomorrow noon for the art school. It seems a bit funny to be going off to school, but I think it is all right. Don't you?"[93] This was an emotional time for him. Because of his age, a state law mandated that he retire from his position as professor and department head. Because Waugh had been dreading his mandatory retirement, it seems logical that he would try something new in this time of transition. He decided to gain new drawing and painting skills with the hope of doing some etching as well.

Waugh selected Charles Woodbury's Ogunquit Summer School of Drawing and Painting, which Woodbury had founded in Perkins Cove in 1898. A brochure from the Ogunquit Museum of American Art describes the attractive powers of Ogunquit:

> "Since the 1890s, Ogunquit has been a destination for artists who sought the camaraderie of fellow artists . . . Perkins Cove, a long-established fishing village, eventually developed into a hub where area artists live and work. Because of this, the cove has been drawn and painted again and again throughout the years . . ."[94]

Earlier, both Waugh and Woodbury had taught art at Dartmouth College in Hanover, New Hampshire. In 1929, Waugh taught Art 60, a popularized introductory course about landscape architecture. Woodbury lectured on drawing and painting to art students in January of 1930. On occasion, Waugh returned to do some consulting about the college landscape, and in May of 1930, gave a lecture about landscape architecture. About eleven months later, Waugh offered another lecture on landscape architecture, nearly overlapping with Woodbury who, during the second half of April 1931, lectured students on drawing and painting. Perhaps Waugh and Woodbury had met during these overlaps in Hanover. Such meetings, in addition to the beauty and camaraderie of Ogunquit, could have influenced Waugh's choice of Woodbury's summer art school.

In Ogunquit, Waugh experienced Woodbury's teaching approach, which differed sharply from his own, which had been direct and analytical. Woodbury outlined his provocative teaching style in his book, *Painting and the Personal Equation,* [95] which Waugh probably would have read. He may also have become familiar with Woodbury's pencil sketches of ten native trees that Milton Bradley in Springfield published in 1905.[96]

Running from July 10, through August 18, of 1939, the school, officially renamed the Woodbury-Ross Summer School that year, included classes by Elizabeth Ward Perkins, George K. Ross, and Ellen Marston Ross.[97] The first week of intensive drawing featured a morning class called "Drawing from Special Motion Pictures Films" by Ms. Perkins. From both memory and direct drawing using motion pictures as prompts, students would learn to inject motion into their lines as they gained confidence in their line quality. The Rosses offered an afternoon class called "Structural Design and the Psychology of Composition," where students learned to think more deeply about composition design. Waugh saw some of the work from this session when he arrived at the school on August 1, with a stack of his etchings to show Woodbury. He directed Waugh to work on improving his drawing and set him off sketching. He expressly advised Waugh to "loosen up" with his drawing style. Waugh participated in the core of the program during the second and third weeks where Woodbury introduced a problem for the day in the morning, offering criticism at noon with work continuing throughout the afternoon. During the week, students often worked in plein air on the large slabs of rocks outside Woodbury's Perkins Cove summer home and studio, which served as the school. On Saturdays there would be "concours" or critiques, where work from the week would be hung and discussed critically, no doubt with the sense of movement, line quality, and overall composition among the topics covered. Waugh heard Woodbury deliver his famous maxim, "Paint in verbs, not in nouns." Woodbury challenged his students "to paint it the way it seems, not the way it looks" according to both grandsons.

During his two and a half weeks in Ogunquit, Waugh did not do any etchings, as he had hoped, only drawings and sketches. Woodbury, known for his paintings and drawings, was a prolific and accomplished etcher, as well. His etchings, many of which he displayed in his studio, were distinguished by the sense of movement conveyed by their lines. Woodbury worked to capture the atmospheric feeling of a place, more than its literal appearance. In this way, Woodbury worked as a true artist—not an illustrator. Woodbury's approach influenced Waugh's drawings and his future etchings.

Under Woodbury's tutelage, Waugh made drawings which later served as the basis for etchings. These drawings apparently included ones of the Perkins Cove fishing village, a typical subject of local postcards. They also included one that was realized in August of 1939 in the etching "Four Hickories, 5x7". Waugh created this etching back at home in Amherst. Woodbury's influence is evident. There is a very clear, simple contrast between the heavier, darker lines that make up the four dominant trees in the foreground and the shrubs in the background. The lines creating the background shrubs are lively, simple, and light in value. Such distinctions and value contrasts show more artistic sophistication than in Waugh's earlier etchings; they seem to reflect Woodbury's animated, looser style.

Very sadly, Woodbury died January 21, 1940, about six months after the end of his summer school. He was also beloved by many fellow artists.[98] Between 1898 and 1940 when the school closed, more than four thousand students had benefited from his acclaimed teaching style. As a tribute to Woodbury, in an article entitled, "Drawing Trees," Waugh wrote:

> "One of the best art teachers I ever knew, the late Charles H. Woodbury, always insisted that in sketching trees his pupils express also their environment. In forestry this would be ecology; in art it is the simple truth; but the artist with his pencil has a great advantage over the forester with his camera when this simple truth is to be recorded."[99]

In his drawings and etchings, Waugh had captured the special interest and beauty of trees without the "cluttered and crowded" electric wires, poles, and billboards, and "ugly irrelevant buildings," that would be hard to avoid in a photograph. Woodbury's message to capture the feel of a place, not the look of it, had begun to influence Waugh's art. As he progressed with his etchings, he dared to experiment with a simple kind of motion in his lines that was not evident earlier. Where earlier Waugh may have based his work quite literally on photographs, his work after Ogunquit showed more of the feeling of place that Woodbury had drawn out of his students. Learning how to see, following Woodbury's artful direction, Waugh was becoming more of an artist.

In July of 1940, Waugh returned to one drawing he had made of Perkins Cove to develop it into an etching. He reached out to a Boston colleague of Woodbury's, the internationally renowned printmaker Arthur Heintzelman, for criticism and help with the etching plate. Heintzelman did so at his Marblehead home over the course of a fortnight for a fee of seventy-five dollars. For the finished print with the title, "Fishing Village," Waugh included the caption, "From a drawing done in Ogunquit, Me., 1939, under direction of Charles H. Woodbury; plate etched under criticism and with the help of Arthur Heintzelman, 1940. This cluster of fishermen's shacks lay under the view of Mr. Woodbury's studio."[100]

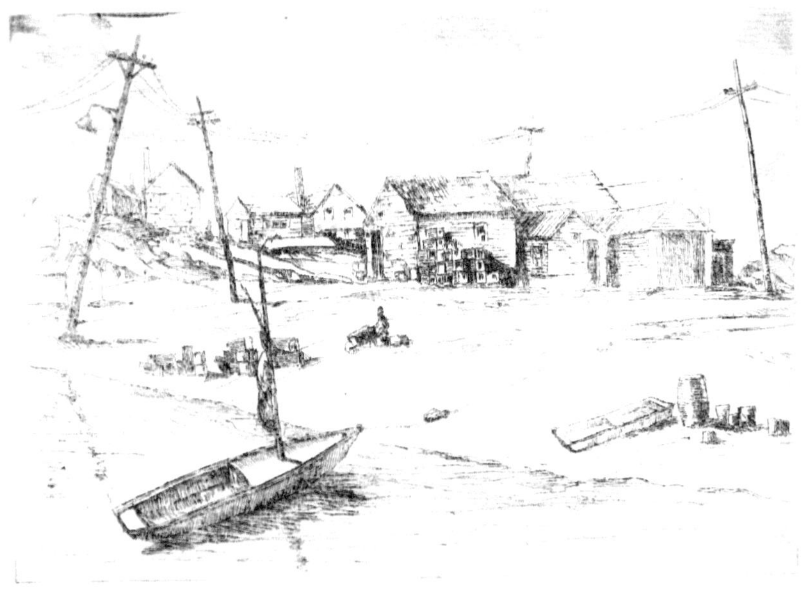

8.1. Waugh, Fishing Village, 5x7, July 1940

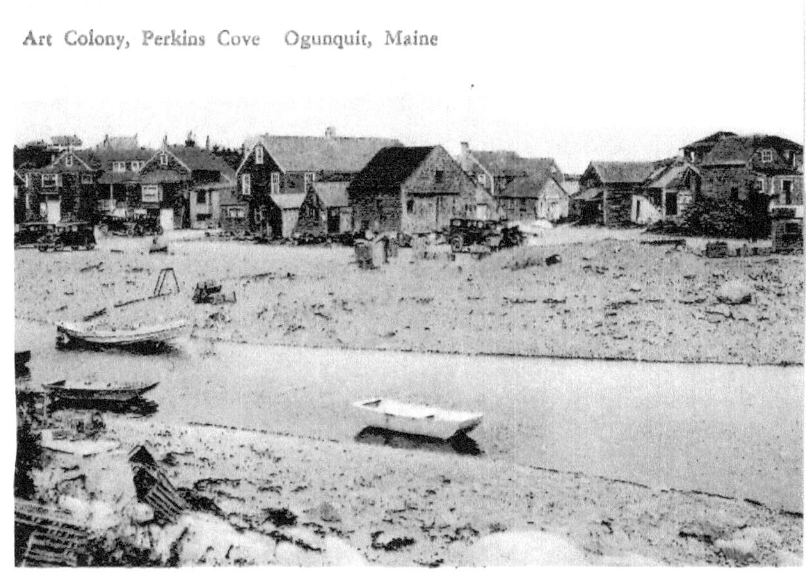

8.2. A post card of the fishing village by the art colony in Perkins Cove, a popular scene in postcards, Author's Collection.

Heintzelman's own etchings favored lively portraits of people, rather than landscapes and trees. His figures seem elastic, full of life with contrasting areas of light and dark. Peers and art historians have noted his debt to Rembrandt.[101] Throughout his career at Massachusetts Agriculture College, Waugh had made photographic portraits of people, presenting exhibits of these portraits at the college. Articles in the *Boston Globe* and the *Christian Science Monitor* noted the success of these photographs in capturing the character of their subjects, a notable achievement then for an academic from the Ag school way out in Amherst.[102] It seems clear that Waugh could appreciate the liveliness of Heintzelman's etchings of people. Yet, the one human character Waugh included in his own Fishing Village etching was stiff and less lifelike.

Waugh wanted his etchings to express the character of trees in ways that a photograph could not. This was evident even before his studies with Woodbury and Heintzelman. In a March 1939 etching based upon photographs and sketches made on the grounds of Cambridge University, elm trees come alive with grace and beauty through lively, though perhaps overworked lines, while the sole female figure looks awkward, stiff, and even stick-like. An etching completed just one year later, based on a single quick sketch that Waugh had done at the edge of a spruce swamp in Maine, shows an even greater degree of abstraction and sophistication, the very "looseness" that Woodbury encouraged. This etching captures the spirit of the trees, representing the essence of a spruce swamp with a simple economy of lively lines.

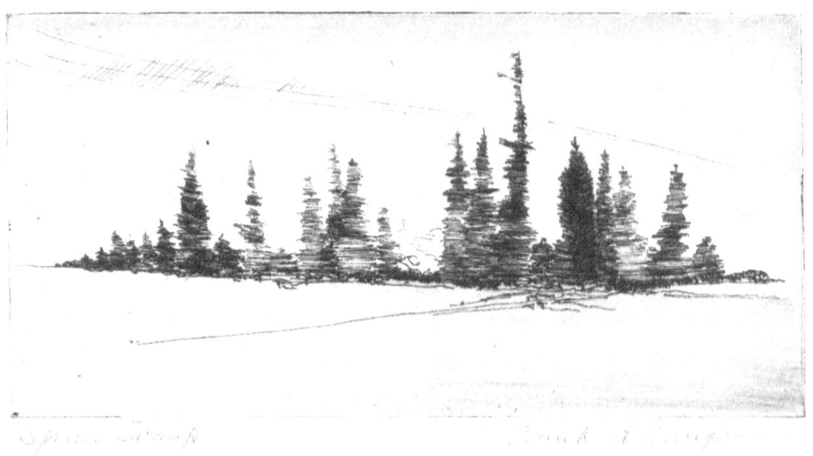

8.2. Waugh, Spruce Swamp, 3x6, August 1940, Author's Collection.

Waugh lost a valued teacher with Woodbury, who had regarded Waugh as one of his most important students.[103] However, Waugh gained a valuable new teacher and critic with Heintzelman, who served as keeper of the prints at the Boston Public Library from 1941 through 1962.[104] Heintzelman's mastery, public networking connections, and savvy would not be lost on Waugh. He taught Waugh not only about developing his own talent, but also something about promoting his own work. Through his studies with Woodbury and Heintzelman, Waugh overcame his dread of retirement very well, while more fully embracing a new avocation, that of printmaking. By September of 1940, his wife arranged a belated birthday present, an etching press of his own, which he set up in his basement.[105] All his etching work could then be completed at home. Ironically, with America's involvement in World War II, Waugh returned to teaching by 1940 to fill in for the colleagues called to service. He devoted his time to teaching, working on the book of trees whose prospectus was introduced in the Prologue, and thinking more and more of himself as an artist in the process.

9

Bringing Beauty to Everyone

The 1930s and early 1940s were a hard time for many Americans suffering from the Great Depression and World War II. Waugh was more fortunate than most. His job remained secure, and he took advantage of his good fortune to devote himself to making etchings. During these bleak times, people sought pleasures they could afford. They could view prints in a gallery or library for free, and many could afford the small cost of a print. Late in his life, Waugh became prolific, making at least 223 etchings between 1934 and 1943. Waugh had numerous exhibitions of his and others' prints and apparently sold some of his own for about two-and-half dollars to five dollars each. Toward the end of this period, Waugh was preparing to publish his popular tree book featuring many of his etchings and drawings.

Waugh and other artists benefited from President Franklin Roosevelt's New Deal programs. The Federal Arts Project of the Works Progress Administration, WPA, supported original printmaking among other artistic endeavors. It subsidized sixteen graphic workshops that provided an opportunity for Americans to create original art. It also supported traveling exhibits that enabled people to see the art and possibly, because of the low printing cost, to buy prints. This support enabled a kind of Renaissance in printmaking in this country and helped Waugh to mount public exhibits of prints and other art at his Massachusetts campus, as well as traveling exhibits of his own work. His daughter Dorothy also benefited directly from this federal support. In 1933, Conrad Wirth had hired her for the State Parks/Emergency Civilian Conservations Works where she designed, as well as supervised production of, posters, stamps, and other graphics intended to encourage people to visit state and national parks.[106]

The MSC also provided Professor Waugh with exhibit space in the Landscape Architecture building, Wilder Hall, as well as in the newly constructed campus buildings Memorial Hall, Curry Hicks, and Goodell Library. In 1936 in a MSC fine art series program, Waugh spoke about the work in an exhibit he hung in Memorial Hall. It featured etchings obtained through one of the graphics workshops the WPA created, the Associated Artists of New York. The local campus newspaper presented an interview with Waugh on the front page:

> "'An etching is like a fine piece of lace or poetry," he said, "to be studied quietly and familiarly. Delicacy and refinement are its outstanding characteristics." Etching, he remarked, lends itself to portraying lyrical and sentimental landscapes, intimate, personal studies of human beings, and subtler effects even to the point of moralization."[107]

In January 1937, when Waugh spoke at Amherst College, he illustrated the steps of making an etching and then shared some of his own etchings, as well as etchings given to the college by Mr. and Mrs. Lucius Eastman.[108] The Mead Gallery at Amherst College today includes a record from 1940 of a purchased etching of Waugh's "Beech Woods."

Waugh also exhibited his etchings off campus. In 1936 Waugh exhibited drawings and etchings of trees and landscapes at the Athenaeum in Westfield, Massachusetts. The front page of the *Amherst Recorder* announced this show and also noted his previous printmaking studies in Eastport.[109] In January 1938 the front page of the *Recorder* featured a story about Waugh's one-person show at The Jeffrey Amherst Bookstore in downtown Amherst. The etchings on display ranged from landscape views of his travels to Fontainebleau, England, California, and Kansas, as well as local landscapes from the MSC campus and surrounding area, featuring such scenes as a cider mill and a sawmill. The article noted that Waugh set out to "make an artistic record of rapidly vanishing aspects of New England life in this region."[110]

It is possible to find accounts of Waugh's own work available as a traveling exhibit. The College of Architecture and Design at the University of Michigan in Ann Arbor announced an exhibit called "Etchings of Trees" by Professor Frank A. Waugh, Massachusetts State College Jan 17-27, 1941, arranged by Professor Whittemore.[111] The 1936 records at the Birger Sandzén Memorial Gallery in Lindsborg, KS, of their *Sandzén Art Register* (12), state, "An exhibition of Mr. Waugh's prints will be available for Kansas State College, Manhattan, and for Bethany College, later in the season. Mr. Waugh is now Oct 1-Nov1 giving an exhibition of his recent work at the Athenaeum in Westfield, Mass."[112] *The Sandzén Art Register* also notes another exhibition of Waugh's etchings with this entry, "February 1-22 Exhibition of etchings and drawings by Frank A. Waugh in 1937." One additional entry about Waugh in the *Register* includes this record, "Bought by Smoky Hill Art Club: Watson's Mill, $5.00, North Leverett" and "Roadside Maples, $5.00" with a further note in the entry "Kept for my own collection, 'Mountain Cabin,' 'Pollard Oaks,' B.S."[113]

A milestone to note dates to February of 1943. The Fine Arts Department of Amherst College loaned thirty works and organized an exhibit from February to March in the Art Room of the Jones Library in Amherst. Among etchings, lithographs, and woodcuts by internationally renowned artists Edmund Blampied, Jared French, Ernest Haskell, Childe Hassam, James McBey, Joseph Pennell, and Chauncey Ryder, Waugh's "Beech Woods" hung as a respected part of the show. Waugh had progressed enough to hang among proven great printmakers. With this coup, Waugh's work could well have been on a path to even more recognition.

Waugh's great hope, apparently, was to publish a volume that would contain a great many of his prints. Although that did not happen, he succeeded in publishing a few articles featuring his etchings. His article from 1938, "Studies from the Nude", emphasized deciduous trees with their bare bones in winter. Etchings of cottonwoods, tupelos, and sugar maples illustrate the article.[114] The next year "Fading Remnant" examined old mills in western Massachusetts, documented in etchings made after the major hurricane of September 1938.[115] And in his 1942 article "Drawing Trees" Waugh advocated etching, as well as drawing, as opposed to photography. Waugh offered:

> "Early and often it has been pointed out that the camera has largely displaced the pencil and the brush for taking the portraits of trees. . . The modern camera is so complete and perfect, so many persons have become expert in its use, and the typographical methods of reproduction have been so enormously improved that that seems to be no place left for the old-fashioned methods of record. Yet all the while some artists and some tree lovers have clung to old-time skills of drawing and painting, believing that they could put something into the picture, literally that the camera was missing. One remembers with a wistful smile the late William Robinson of England, voluminous writer on trees and gardens, who would never allow his magazine nor his books to be illustrated with photo-halftones, insisting rather on woodcuts painfully hand-made by competent artists. One remembers, too, with thanks, the beautiful etchings of native trees done by such eminent American artists as Alfred Hutty, W.R. Locke, and Hans Kleiber. Prints like theirs have an

esthetic appeal wholly different from the best photographs and, in a way, superior to them."[116]

Waugh concluded with these thoughts:

"I have myself photographed trees almost the world over for more than fifty years, and I consider the camera indispensable. The only answer is that we want both. We want the best possible photographs of trees everywhere; but we also want good paintings and drawings done by artists who know these media and who-and this is very important-also know their trees. For an artist, to draw trees in the way we are asking, must be a close student of this subject and above all an intimate lover of trees. We all hope that everyone who has anything to say in praise and admiration of trees may be encouraged to say it freely, using his full vocabulary, whether through the medium of poetry, painting or photography."[117]

While it was easy to get his articles published, Waugh's great hope for his tree book remained a never-successful struggle during the years of World War II. There is evidence that his daughter Dorothy helped him with some aspects of book preparation by providing feedback and advice, and likely more. While his wife, Alice, was away at Kansas State College receiving an honorary master's degree in the fabricated field of "family life" on May 26, 1942, fifty years after her graduation, Frank Waugh wrote to Dorothy, probably on May 31, 1942:

"I will try to send you with this a letter from Mr. Pearce of Duell, Sloan and Pearce, who asked to see my MS but who, like the others, doesn't want to risk its publication in these times. I am going to write him to deliver the MS to you at 38E38. If you don't want to make any use of it for the next few months I think you had better send it by express collect to me, as I can take good care of it in the Wilder Hall safe. But if you want to do any editing now is your chance. The sky is the limit. Go as far as you like. If some of the chapters have to be rewritten you must send them, with your corrections, back to me and I'll have my girl make copies. And if now, or later, you want to offer it to any publisher, go ahead and do it. I'm going to keep trying; but now you may have a turn, if you want it.

It has been offered to Columbia University Press, who promised to publish it, had me make a lot of additions, kept it three years, and then sent it back. Somewhat the same thing happened, with less delay, with the University of NC press. I also tried it on Yale University Press (and) on Macmillan, with no results except kind words and refusal.

I think I will send you, as soon as I can get to it, a print of my latest etching, made this week. 'Woodbury's Sugar-Woods.' I think it is pretty good, but I am still working on it."[118]

And in a subsequent Sunday morning letter after Alice returned from Kansas (suggesting June 7, 1942) Waugh thanks Dorothy for special paper and follows up about the manuscript:

"The Strathmore paper that you gave me proves to be very fine. It is far the best paper that I ever ran a pen over. I made one good drawing and two poor ones on it. Also made a poor etching this week. Now I've got to get busy and do some writing. Please notify me if and when Mr. Pearce sends that MS to you, and let me know if there are any charges.[119]

Waugh did use her gift of fine paper for drawings that seem to be candidates for the book, including those presented in the current portfolio. It is not known whether Dorothy received the manuscript itself, and there's no trace of what happened to it. In another undated letter written sometime in June of 1942, Waugh reveals the kind of advice and help he sought from his talented, artistic daughter. Especially during World War II, with son Sidney Waugh off to assignments, Dorothy became the valued source of expert opinion:

"I'm mailing you under another envelope a drawing of some palm trees that seems to have gone sour. Mamma doesn't like it, but can't give much of any reason why. She says she thinks the trees at the right lean backward and they don't look so straight and solid as palm trees should. I don't like the drawing either, and I don't know the reason why much better than Mamma does. I would throw it in the waste basket without regret except that I think I see some promise in it. I just thought you might be able to straighten me out. Tell me what's the matter with it; but if it is something that can't be corrected throw it away at once. Or if you see some other way to do it better I would just as soon make another drawing. Don't hesitate to retouch it yourself in any way that pleases you. But don't waste much time on it; it isn't worth it.

I'm plugging along on this and some other drawings and doing a little writing for the same book. But the weather is very nice and I'd rather go riding with my Master of Family Life if I had plenty of {gasoline} gasolene."[120]

And it is clear that Waugh valued the help of his cherished wife, Alice, in the preparation of the etchings intended for the book:

"Mamma and I have had two sessions this week with the etching press and have made some very good prints. It is a great advantage to have Mamma's help. But I have been so busy with my classes and other college work, that I haven't touched any new work on any etching for nearly a month."[121]

An interesting point that becomes clear and helps give a context of date comes from the following excerpt, where Waugh noted that he was back teaching, due to shortages in staff as a result of the war:

> "This afternoon Mamma and I printed several etchings, all from the one plate, "October Haze." It is a great help when Mamma comes in. She keeps her hands clean and handles the paper. When I work by myself, with my hands all ink, I can't help smooching every print, putting it into the press or taking it out, usually both.
>
> I haven't done any etching for two or three weeks now. I find that my teaching keeps me pretty busy. And there are always some other things to do"[122]

This "October Haze" etching may well have become renamed "November Haze," with a specific date of September 1942. Certainly, these were hard times, with so many men away at the war in the 40's, and times of paper shortages when publishers were hesitant to commit to new projects. There were also times of gasoline shortages, where people had to think carefully about what trips they could afford to take. Yet during these challenges, Waugh returned to his beloved college work, without financial compensation, and at the same time advanced his art dramatically. Waugh was on his way to realizing more success with his trees in the landscape when he developed pneumonia, passing away March 20, 1943.

What additional success might he have achieved? Sadly, no one ever published his tree book. The manuscript seems to have been lost. Scholars do not seem to know about it. But, as already described, a prospectus for his book with a long list of proposed illustrations turned up in September of 2019 in a box at an antiques store in Palmer, Massachusetts, including a sheet of handwritten proposed titles with a check next to "Tree Portraits." Many of the etchings and drawings in a tall stack inside the fruit crate were on the proposed illustration list. Because Waugh's writing style was deemed old-fashioned even in his time, his books might not hold much appeal for the public today. Yet, the extensive tree images Waugh created near the end of his life seem timeless. Through these lovingly created illustrations, Waugh leaves a visual legacy that readers can view in the following gallery. In these well considered views of trees, Waugh captured their beauty for us.

10

A Gallery of Trees

Waugh hoped to have more than ninety illustrations of trees in his book. One typed list of trees found with the prospectus listed ninety-four trees by their common name. This list includes some notes in Waugh's handwriting about which trees might be full page with suggestions for others as "thumbnails." Included in the box with his typed prospectus entitled *Portraits of Trees, Project for a Book*, was an undated scrap of plain newsprint. On this Waugh had written the following list in pencil: "A Tree Book, A Book of Trees, Tree Portraits, The Beauty of Trees, Trees for Beauty, How Trees Look, An Artist Looks at Trees, and Tree Personalities." Next to the third item, "Tree Portraits," was a check mark in red ink. Whether Waugh intended *Portraits of Trees* or *Tree Portraits* for his final book title is not clear. All the titles he considered for his book share the goal of getting people to appreciate trees. In the prospectus, Waugh noted that he preferred etchings for his illustrations, listing pen drawings second, ("These seem to be effective and easy to reproduce,") third pencil drawings ("a few") and fourth photographs ("*ad libitum*"). His granddaughter Margaret recalled that F.A.W. first took up etching so that he could capture trees in that medium. And he had this book project in mind then.[123]

Trees on the list for this gallery range widely in geography from east to west, north to south. Settings vary from city to farm, forest to field, riverside to mountain top. Some scenes include streets, walkways, fences, walls, and gates. Others feature native landscapes. Although the locations of all the listed trees are not always known, each one is from a specific place. Some compositions feature the tree in a minimal setting. For others, especially in later etchings, Waugh developed an elaborate sense of space and more tonality through a distinct foreground, midground and background. Waugh carefully presents the character of trees in a variety of compositions, recalling his own design principles and views on grouping.

These works are presented following an organization Waugh used in his handwritten lists of etchings—single specimen vs. groups of trees. Adopting that system for this gallery, the first ten examples feature single specimen trees. Next come trees in groups of two, then three, followed by four, and finally larger groups. The drawings and etchings show a wide cross section of the very illustrations Waugh created for his now lost book. The names of each work are those Waugh provided. Locations and dates, if known, are noted. Sometimes that information was written on the mount of the drawing or etching. The sizes of the drawings are given as the sheet size. No list of drawings by Waugh has yet been uncovered, but Waugh did compile a complete list of his etchings which appears in the Appendix. The size of each etching refers to the original plate size, as recorded by Waugh, together with notes about the type of etching and its condition, if available. These selections form an introduction to the prolific body of significant artwork Waugh created in the last seven years of his life; they contribute very tangibly to his enduring legacy. Waugh's demonstrated success with aquatint, which his French etching teacher Ouvré had shown him earlier, can be seen in the last two etchings here, "Tulip Trees" and "November Haze." Captions to the following plates provide the dimensions in inches.

May the reader enjoy this small, but choice collection of Waugh's trees.

Frank Waugh Etchings and Drawings

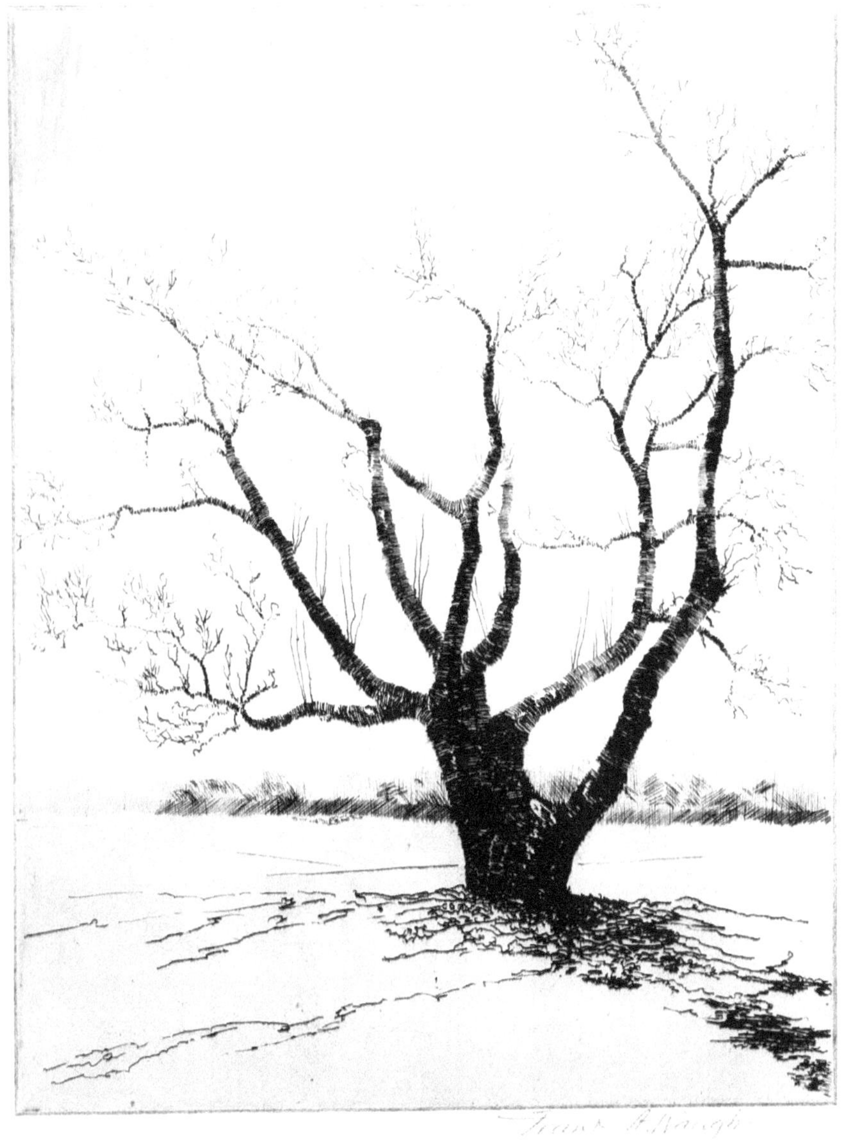

1. Old Apple Tree, 9x7, etching, Dec. 1937

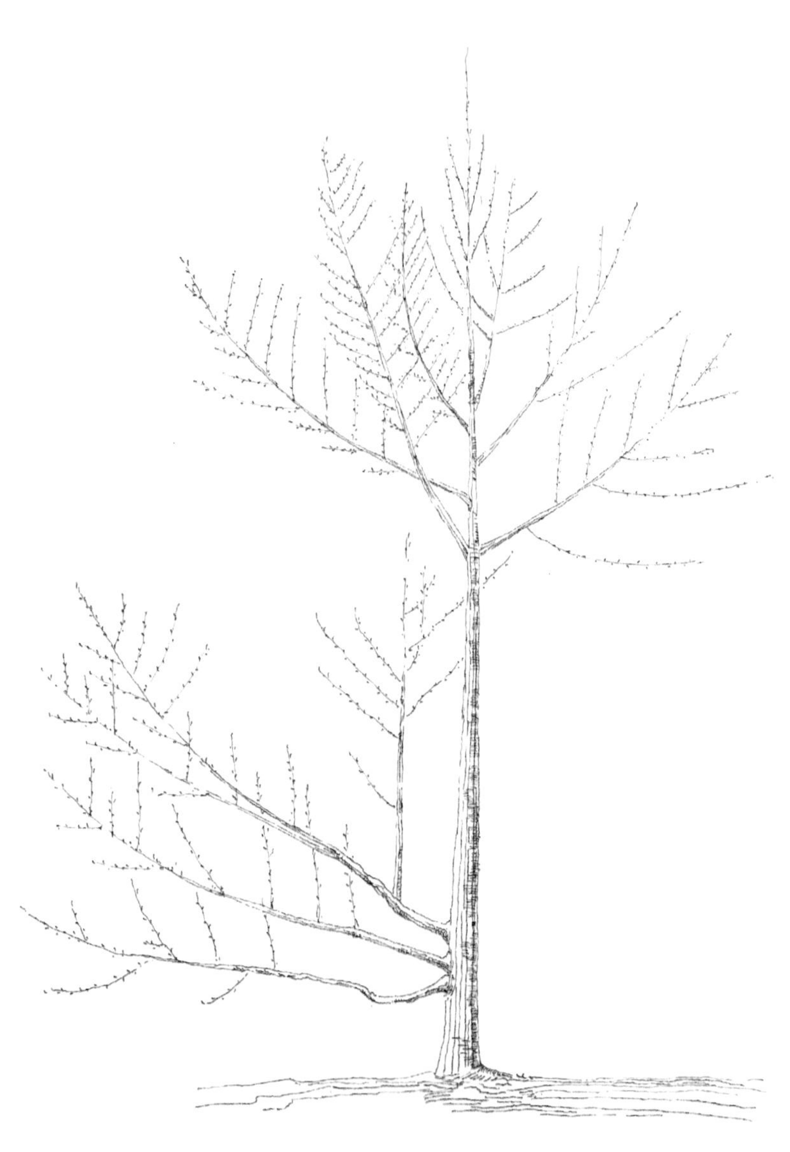

2. Ginkgo, deformed by crowding, 12x9, pen, date from note on back as May 1940

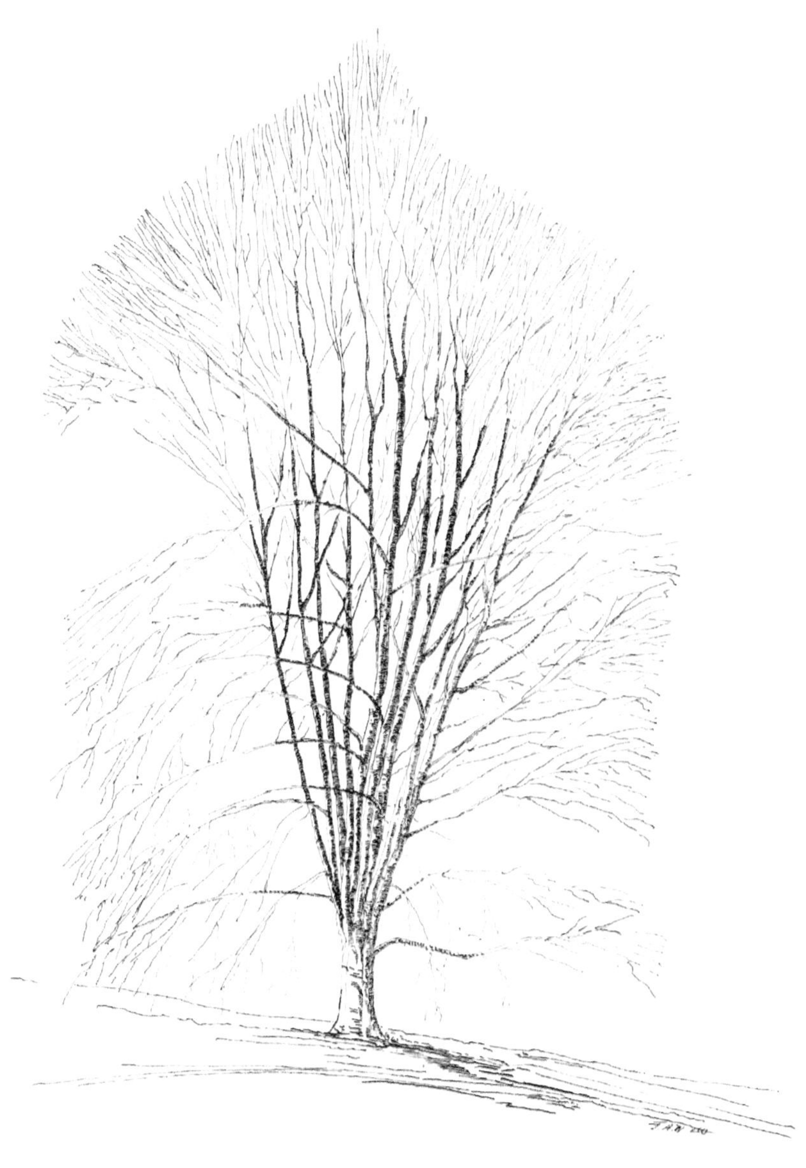

3. Bigleaf European Linden, Tilia platyphyllos, 12x9, pen, 1940

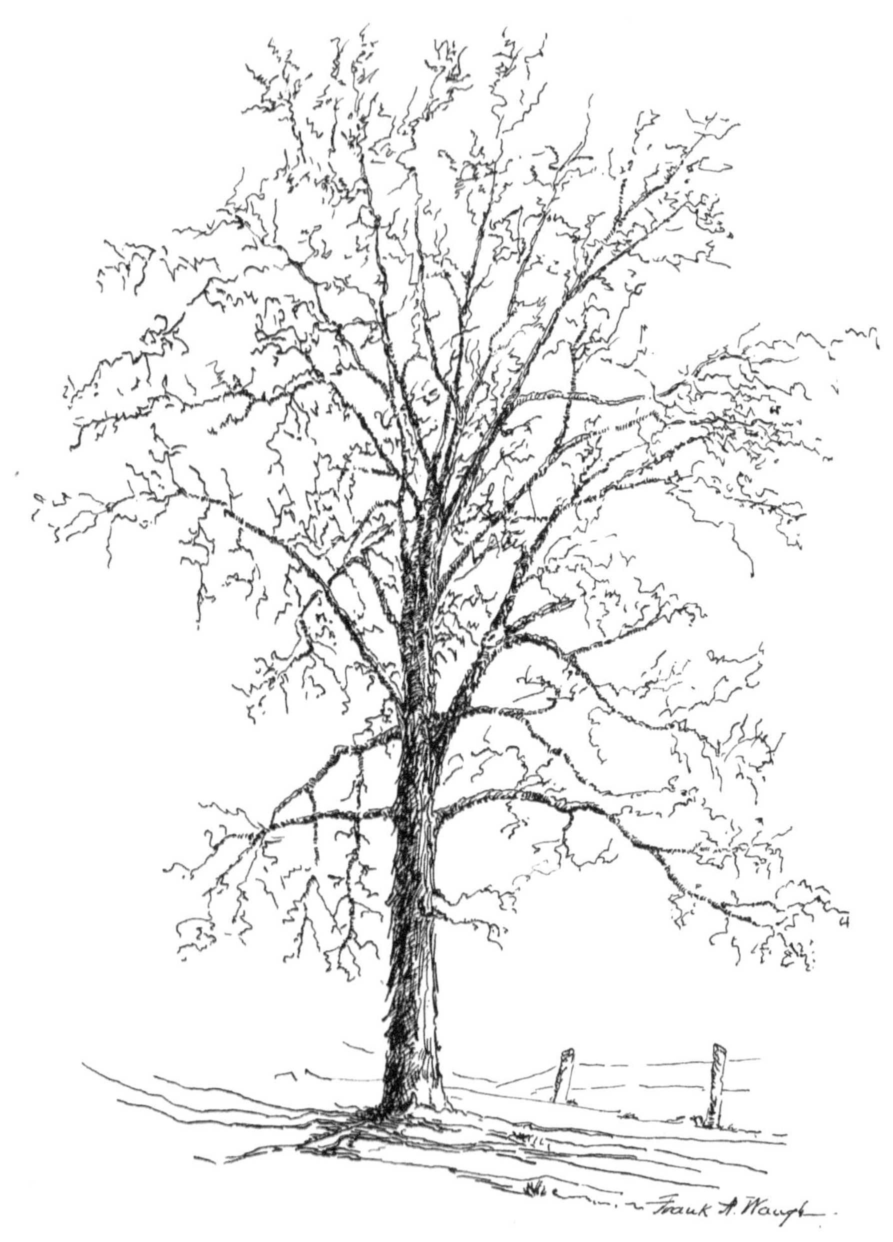

4. Hickory in November, 12x9, pen

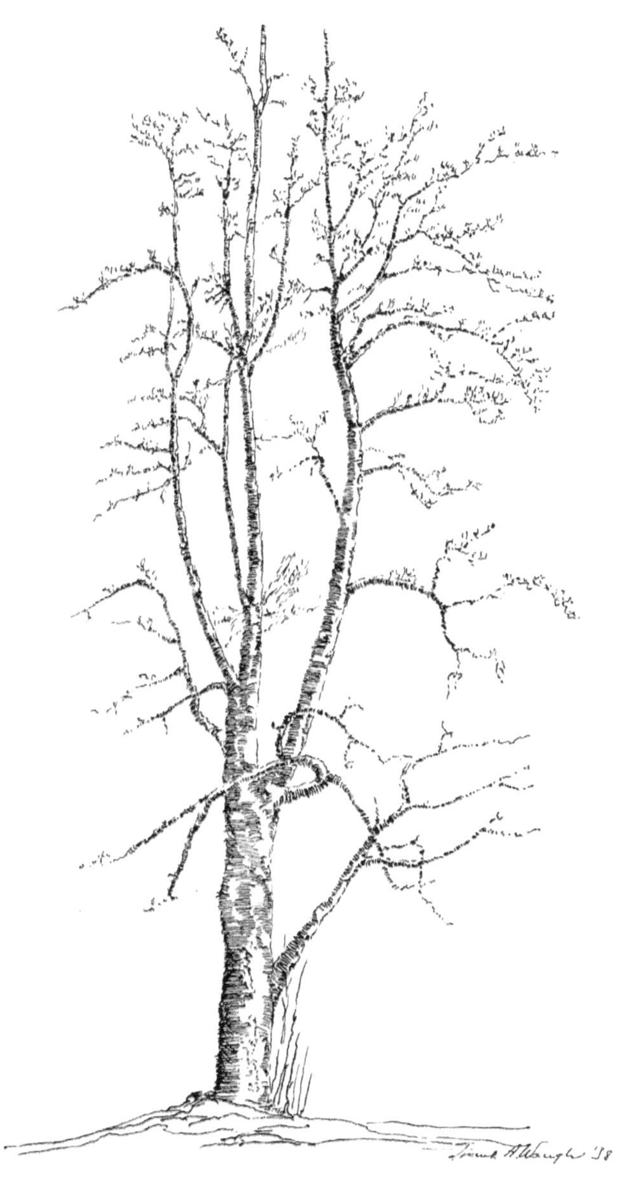

5. Sheldon Pear, 12x9, pen, 1938

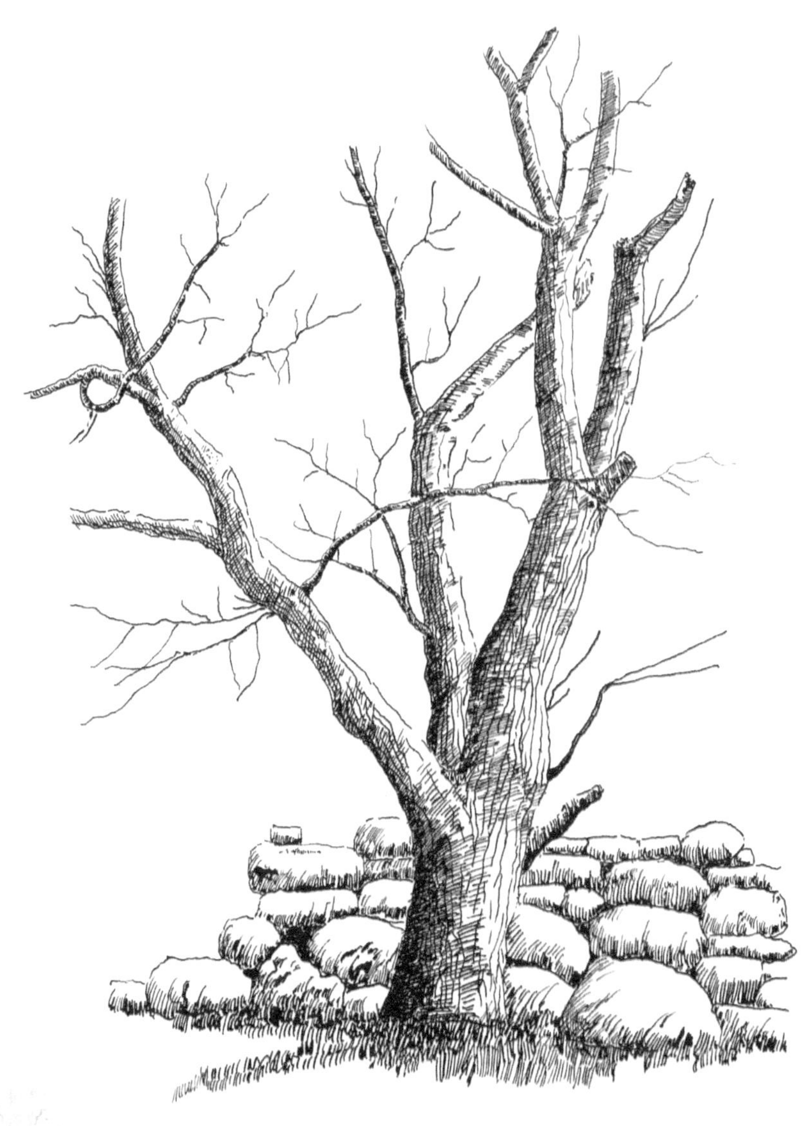

6. Butternut, 12x9 (note on Strathmore), pen

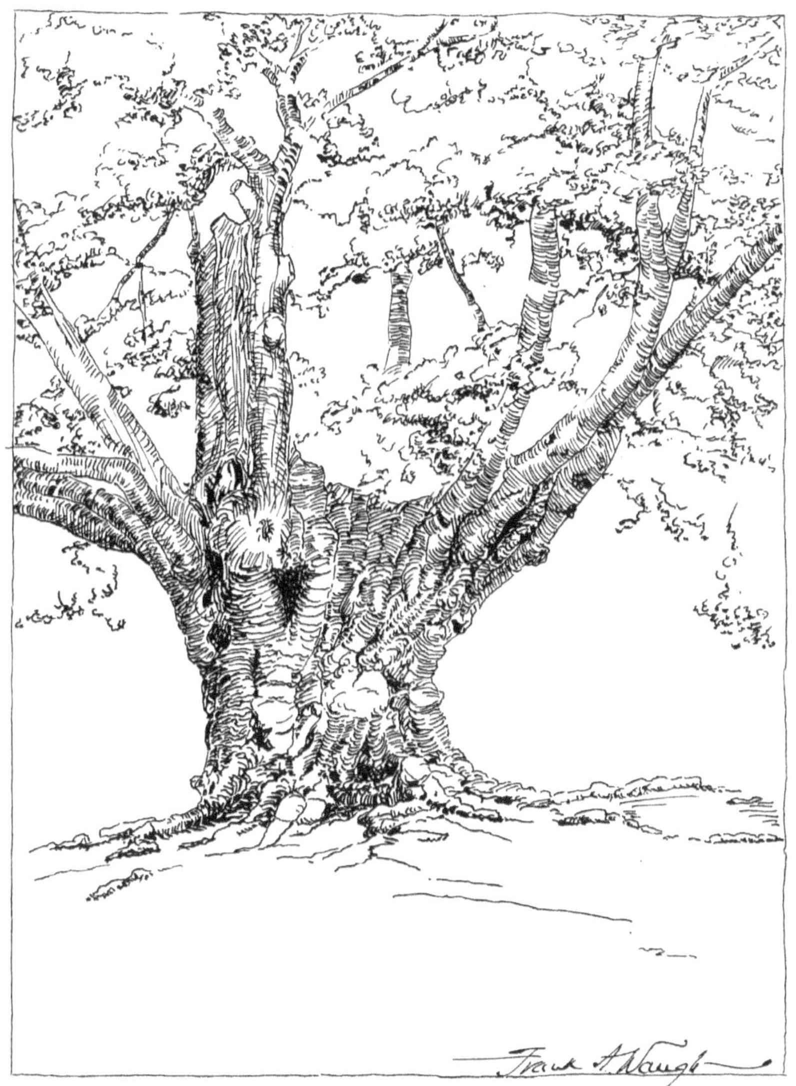

7. Burnham Beeches, 18x12, pen

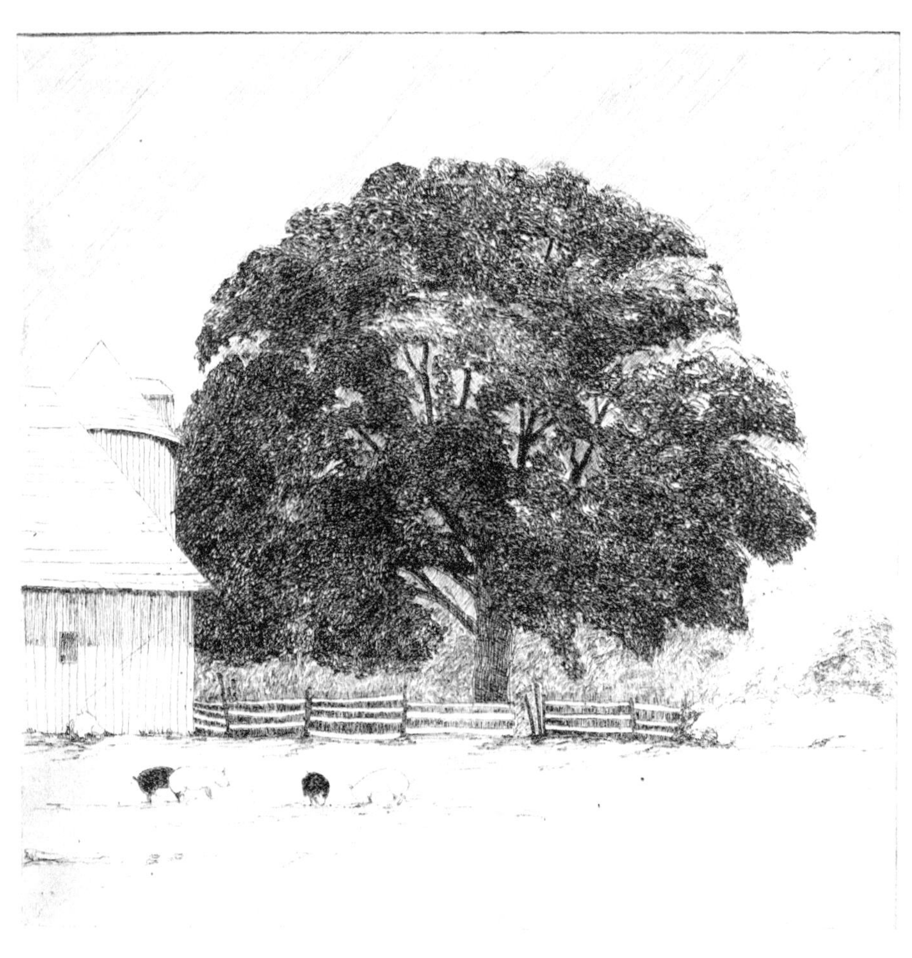

8. Barnyard Oak, 8x8, etching, June 1941

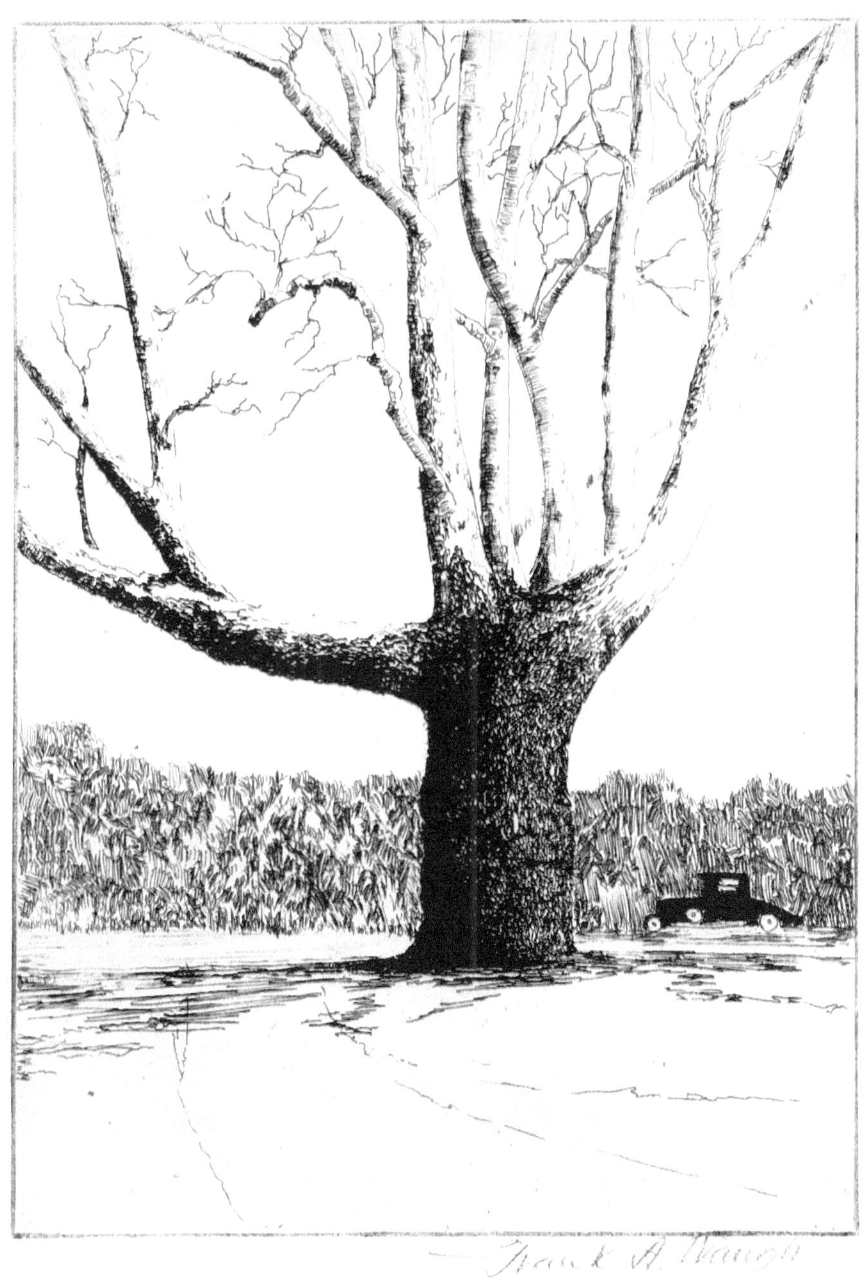

9. Big Sycamore, Sunderland, MA, 7x5, etching, Apr. 1938

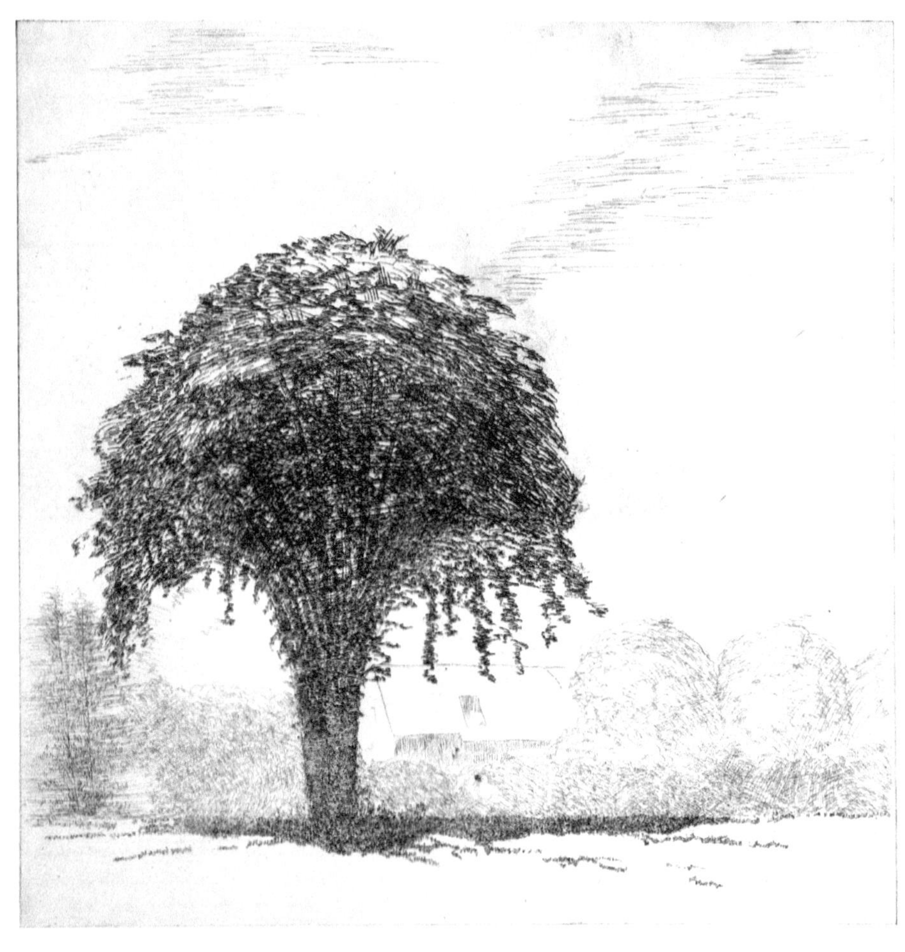

10. David Grayson's Elm, Amherst MA, 8x8, etching, Jul. 1942

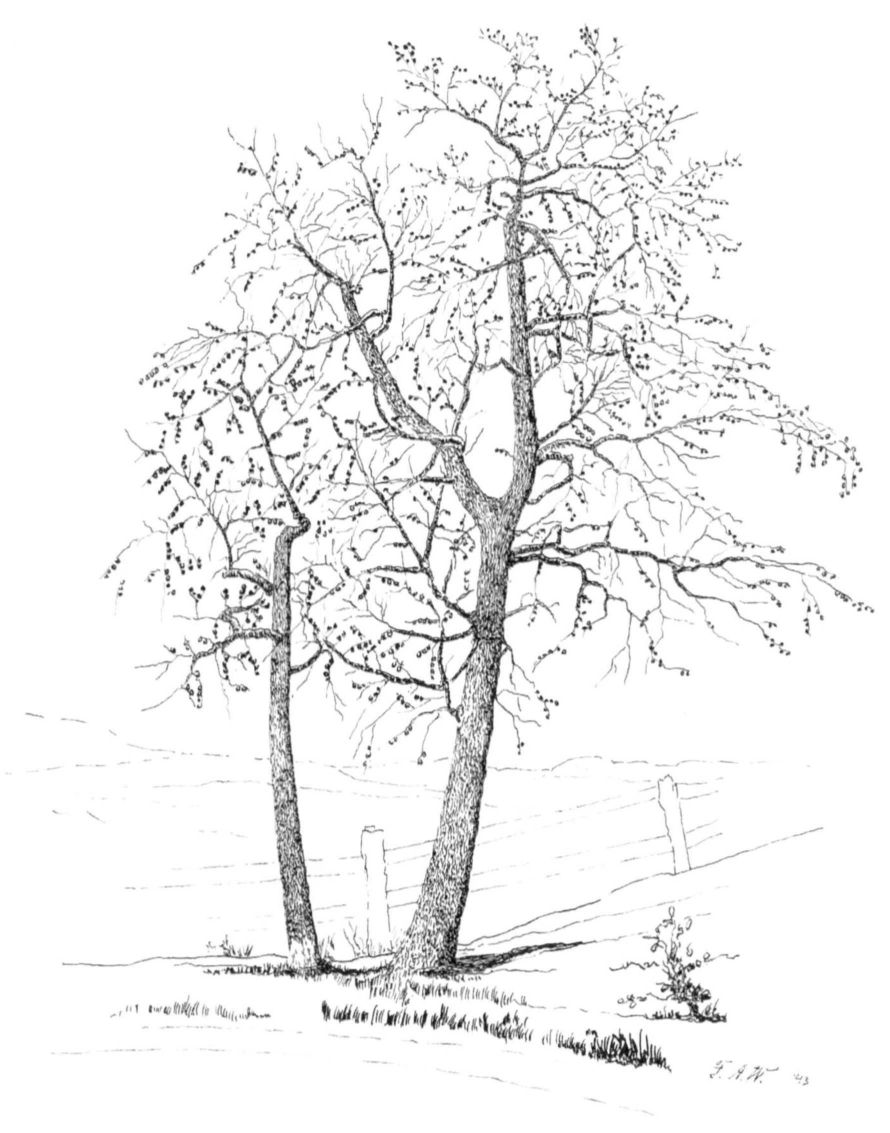

11. Persimmons, 12x9, pen, 1943

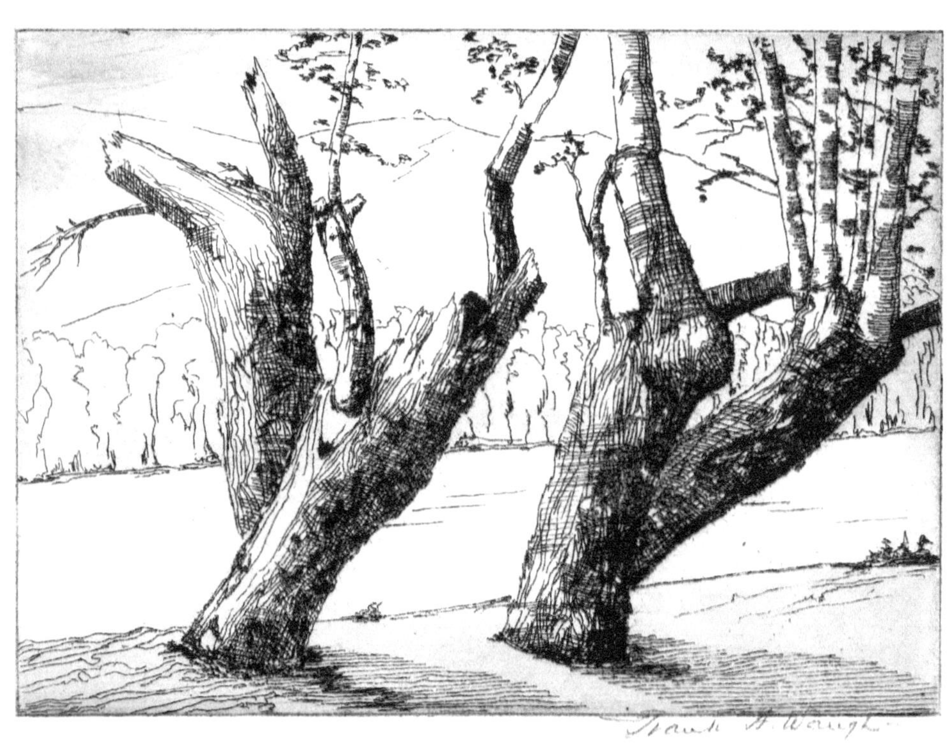

12. Cottonwoods, Virgin River, Utah, 5x7, etching, Jan. 1937

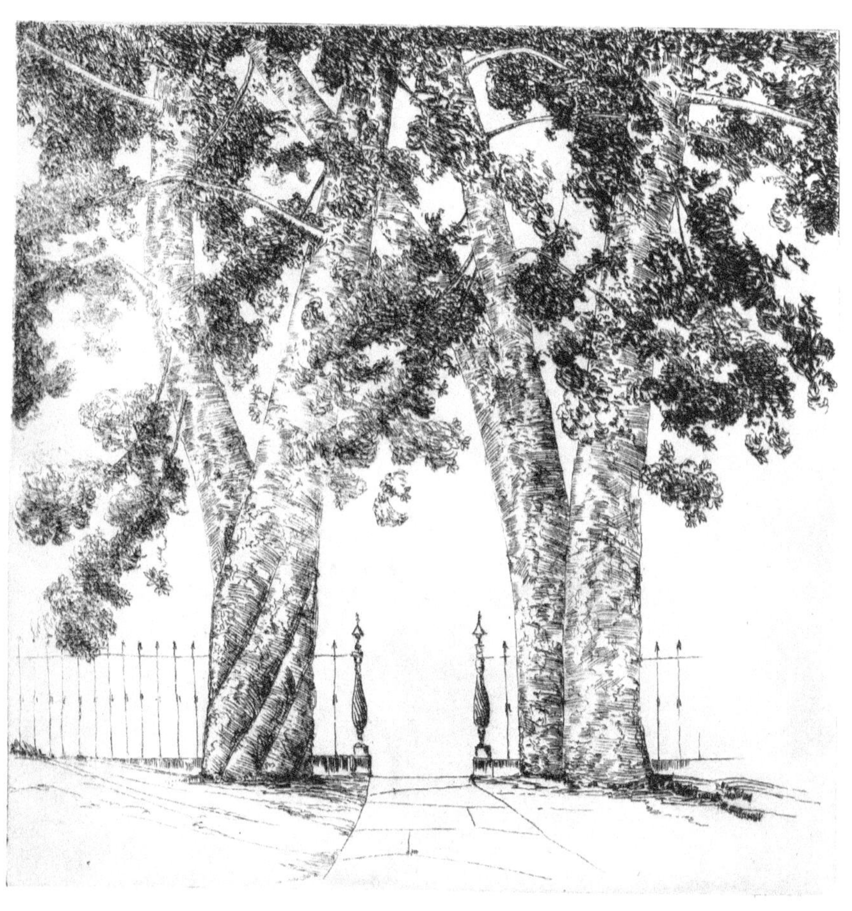

13. The Gate (Horse Chestnuts), 8x8, etching, Nov. 1940

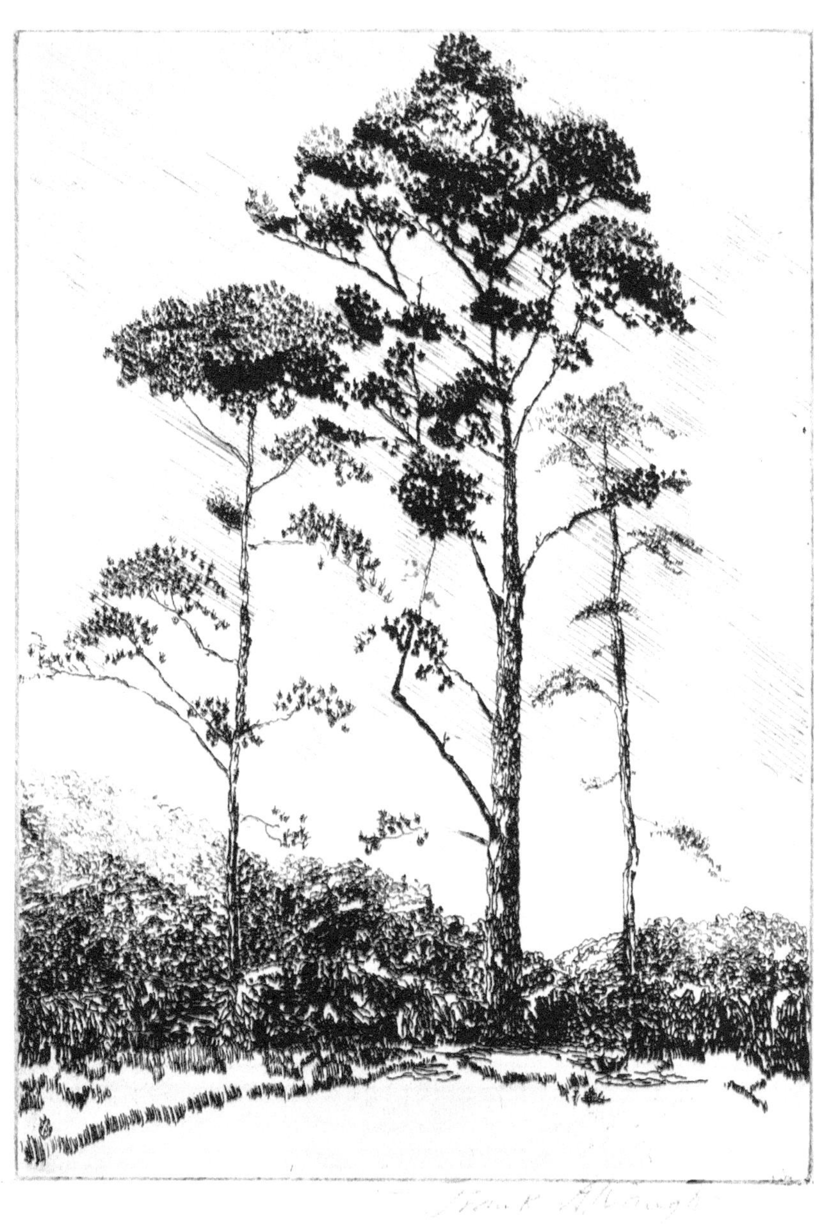

14. Pitch Pines, Cape Cod, 7x5, etching, Sep. 1939

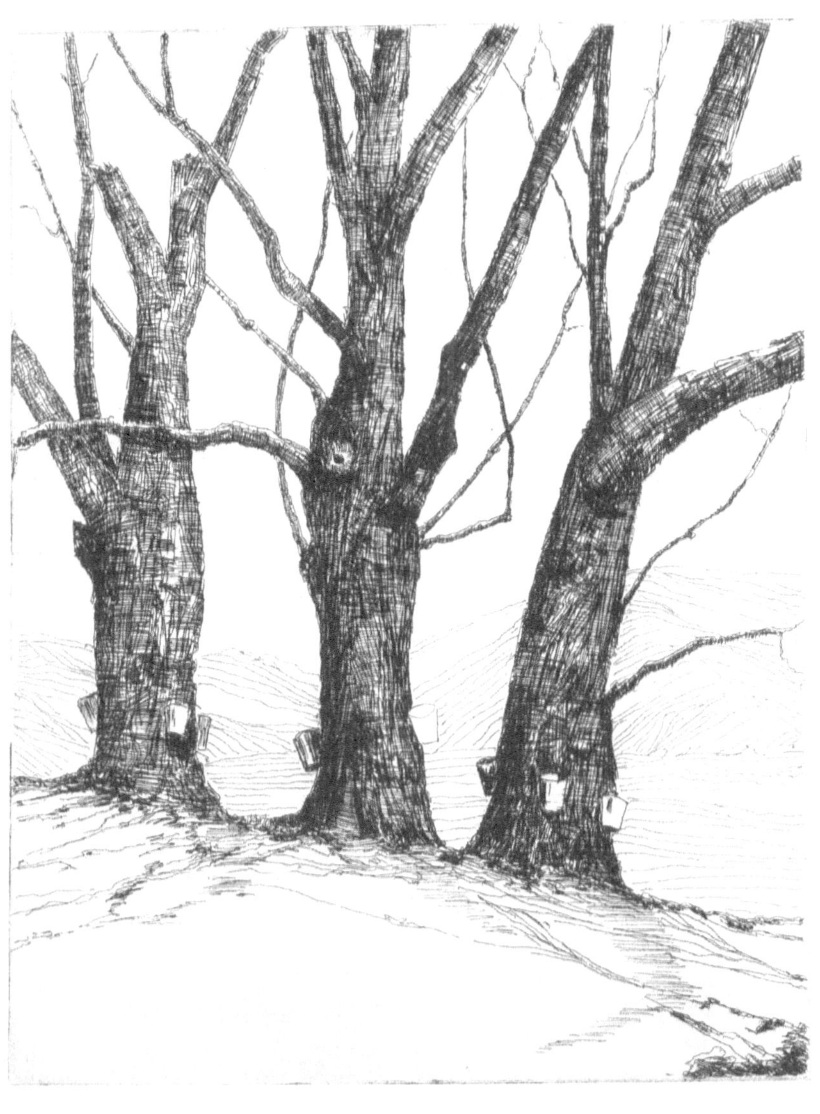

15. Sugar Maples, Sunderland, MA, 7x9, etching, Mar 1937

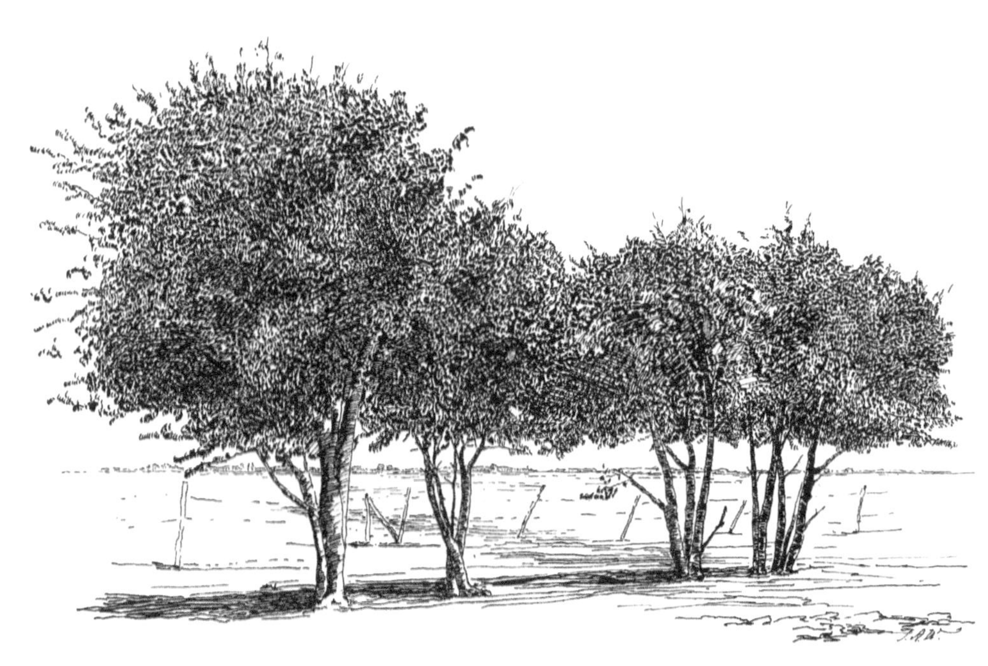

16. Osage Orange, 9x12, pen, 1941

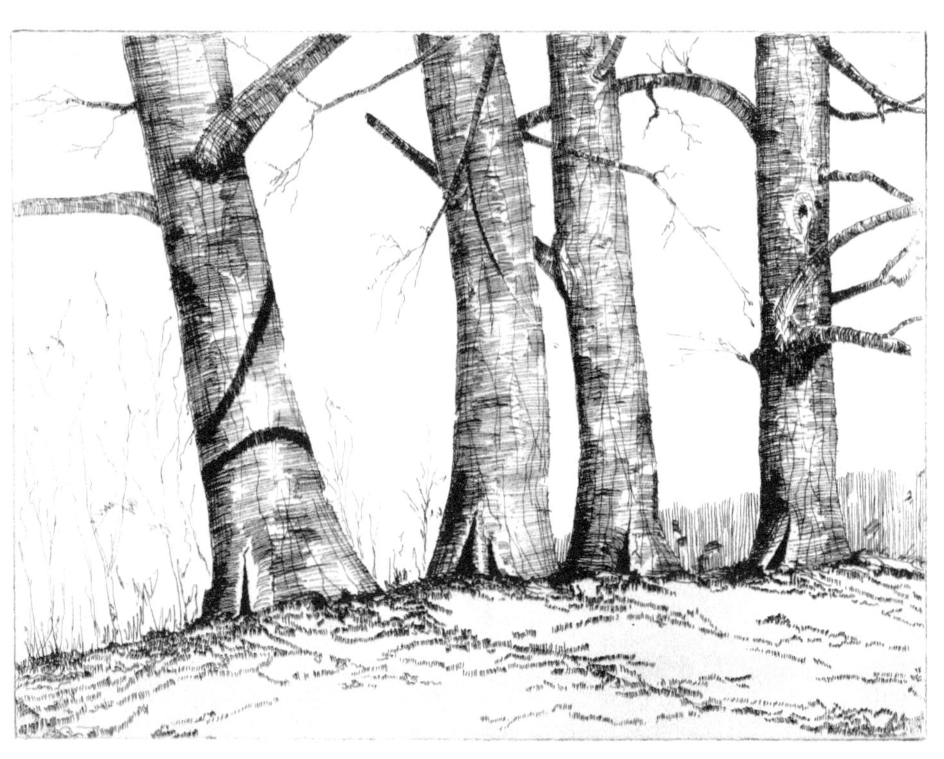

17. Chestnut Boles, 6x8, etching, Dec. 1936

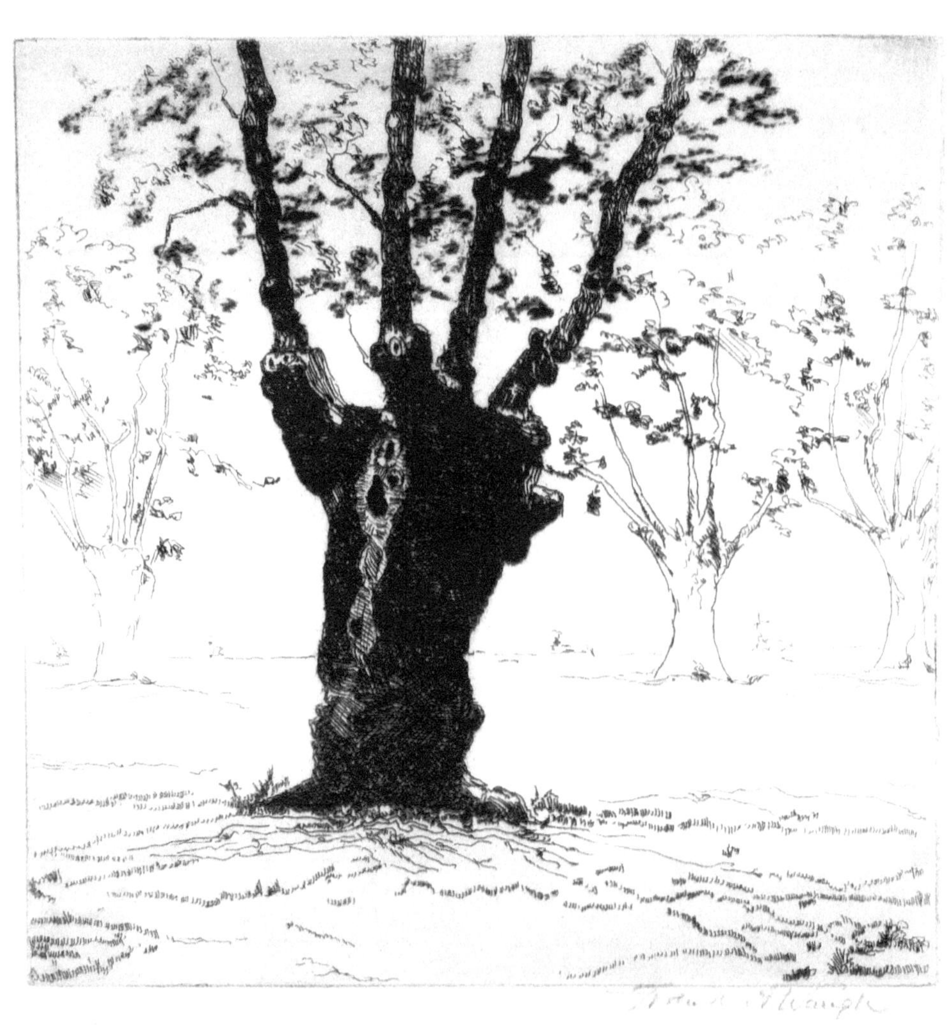

18. Pollard Oaks, Epping Forest (London, England), 6x6, etching, Sep.1936

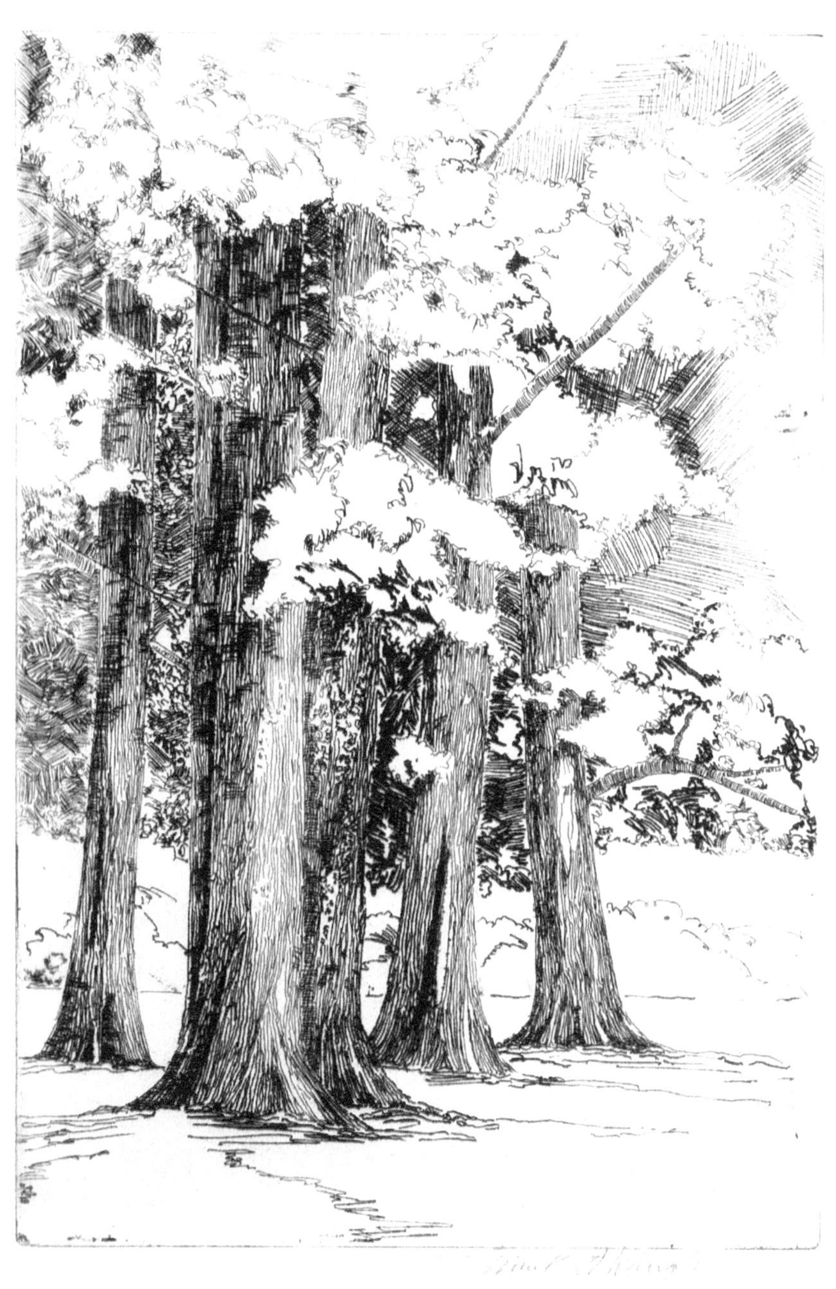

19. Cryptomerias, Nara, Japan, 8½x6, etching, May 1938

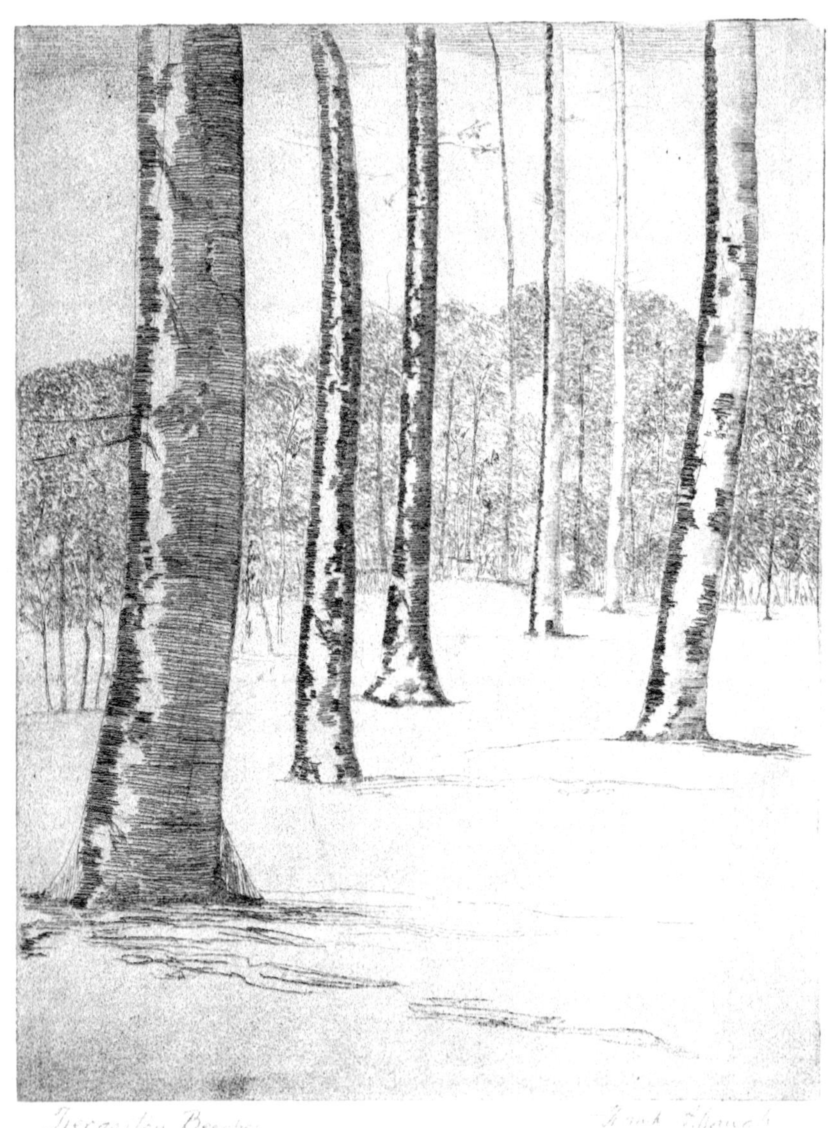

20. Tiergarten Beeches, Berlin, 8½ x6½, etching, Apr. 1942

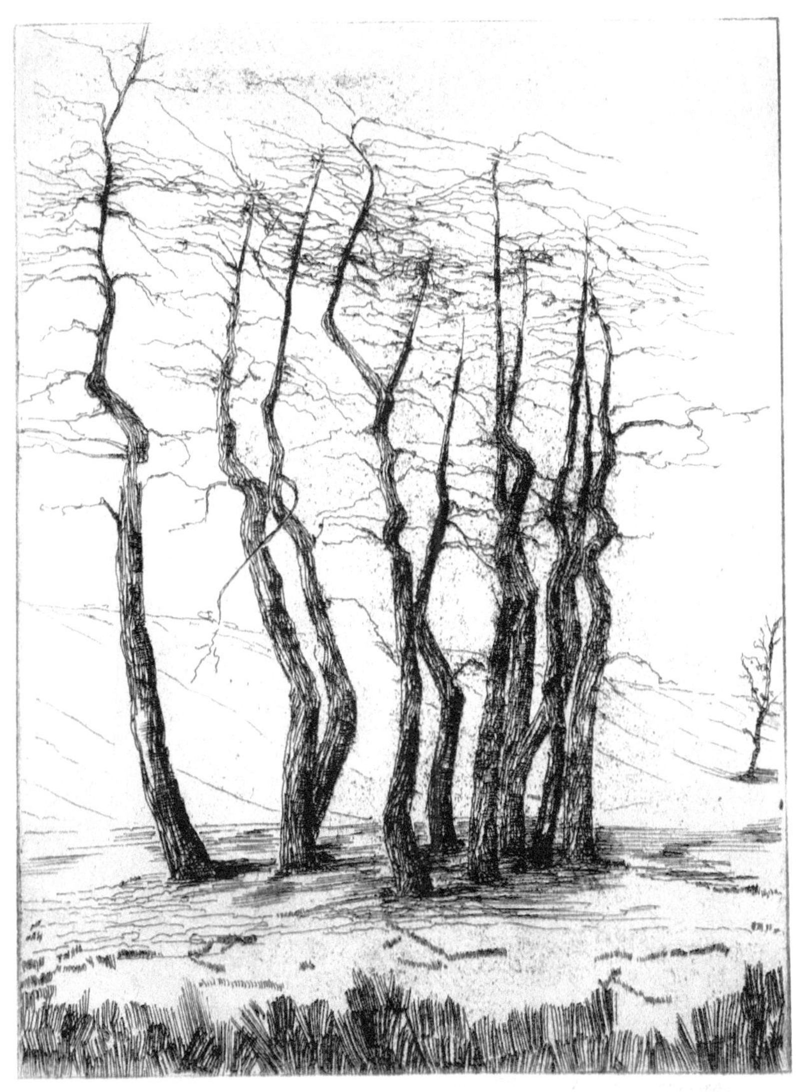

21. Tupelos, Fisher's Island, 8x6, etching, Apr. 1937

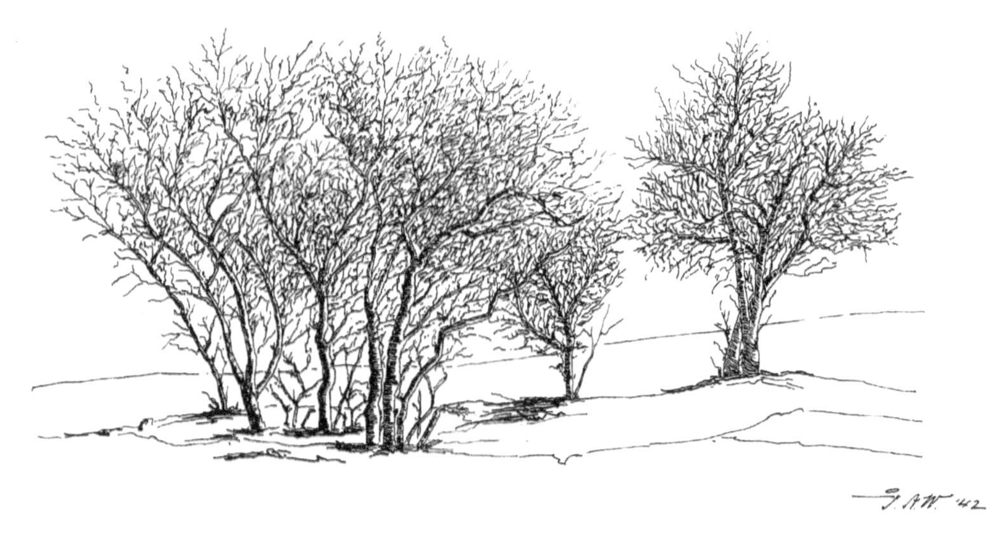

22. Wild Plums, 9x12, pen, 1942

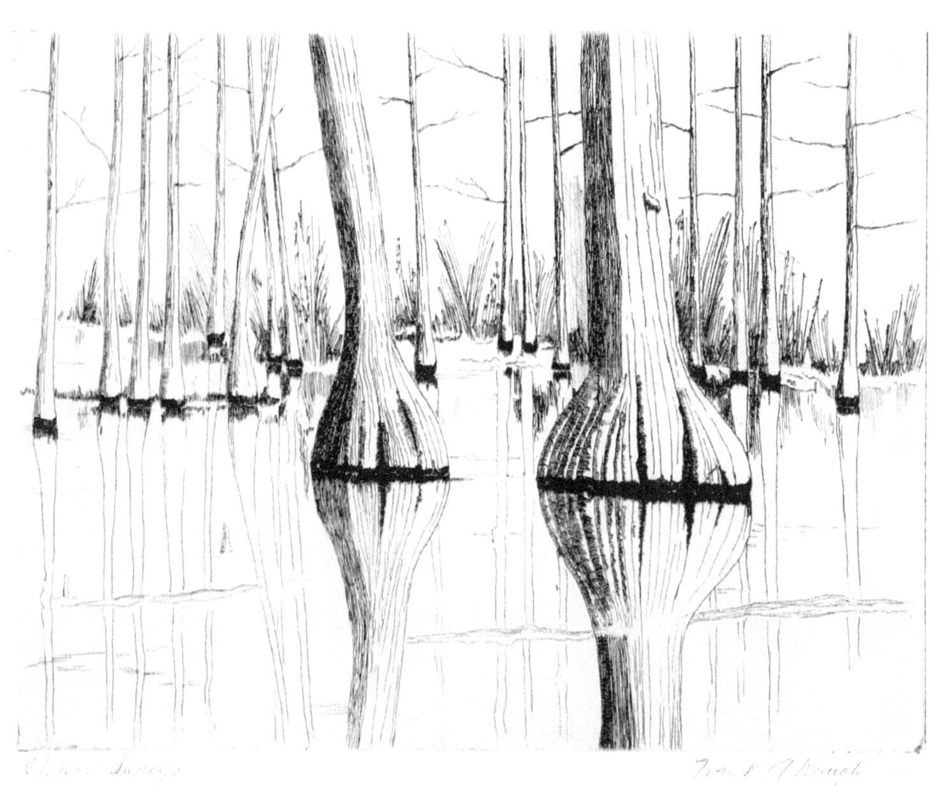

23. Cypress Swamp, Florida 6½x8½, etching, Apr. 1940

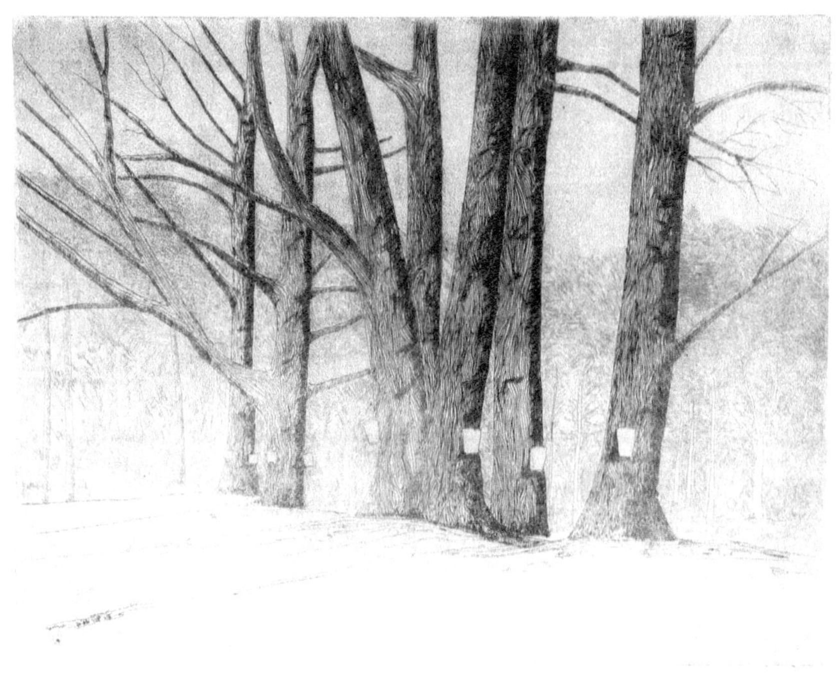

24. Woodbury's Sugar Woods, 6½x8½, etching, May 1942

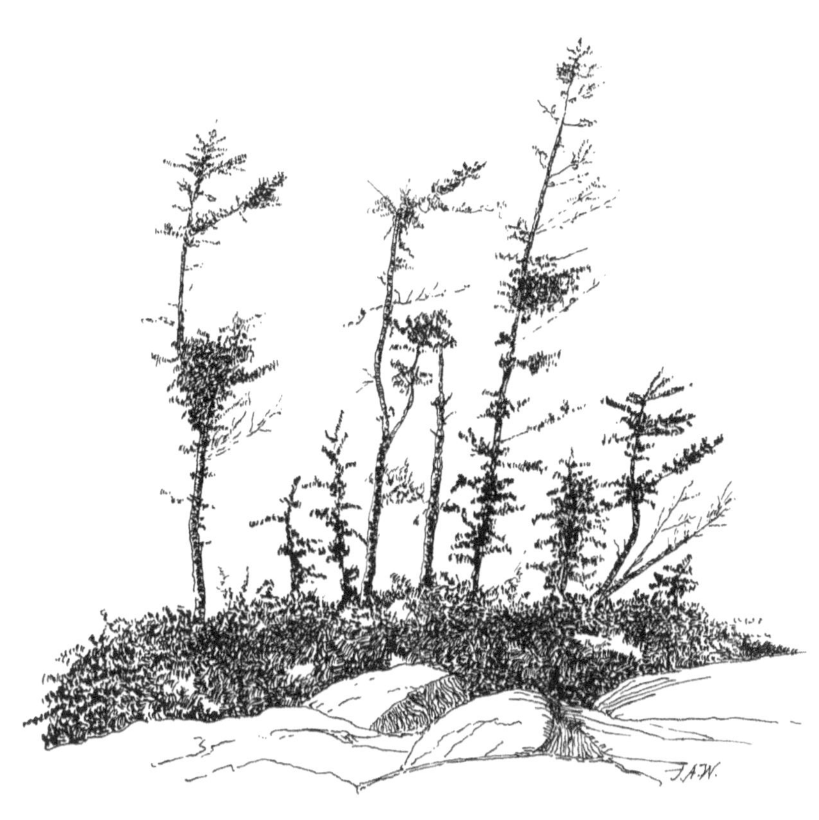

25. Spruce on the Summit of Mt. Cadillac, 8.5x7, pen, 1940

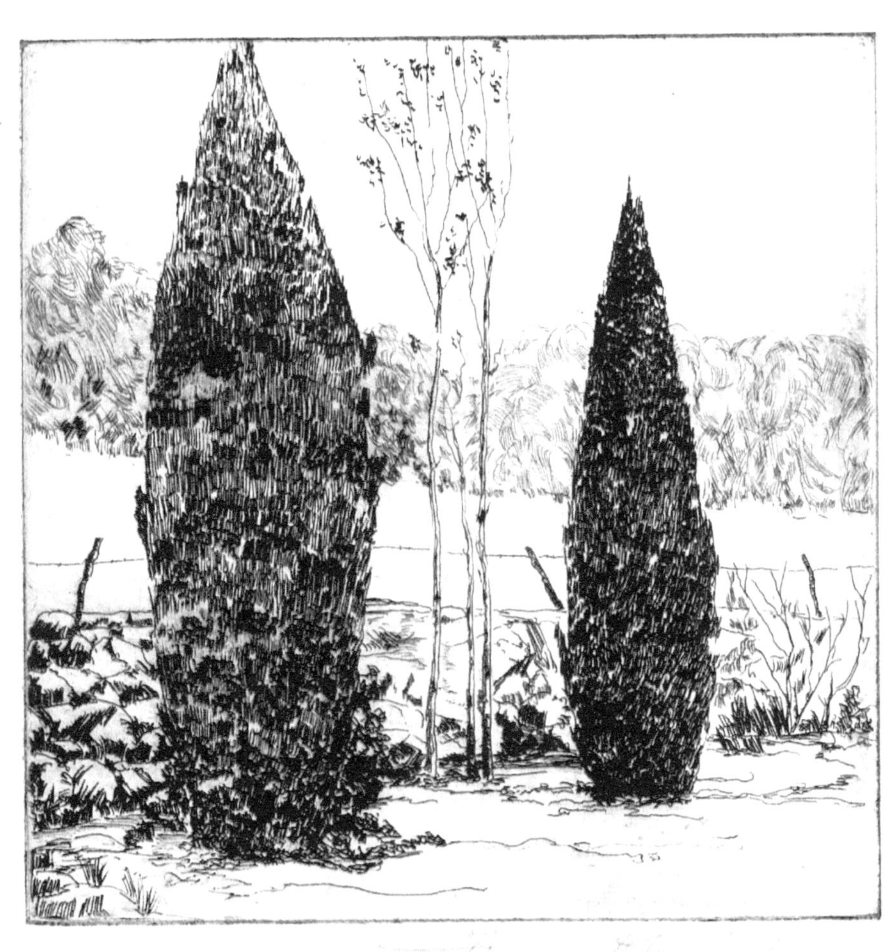

26. Cedars and Birch, 4 x4, etching, Jul. 1940

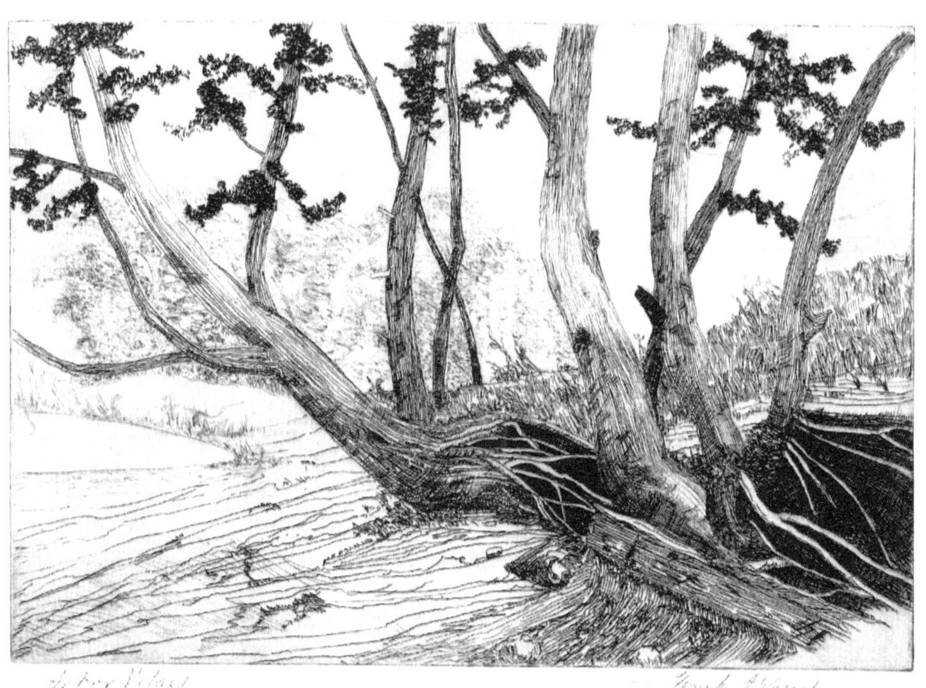

27. Arbor Vitaes, 5¾x 8 ½, etching, Oct. 1940

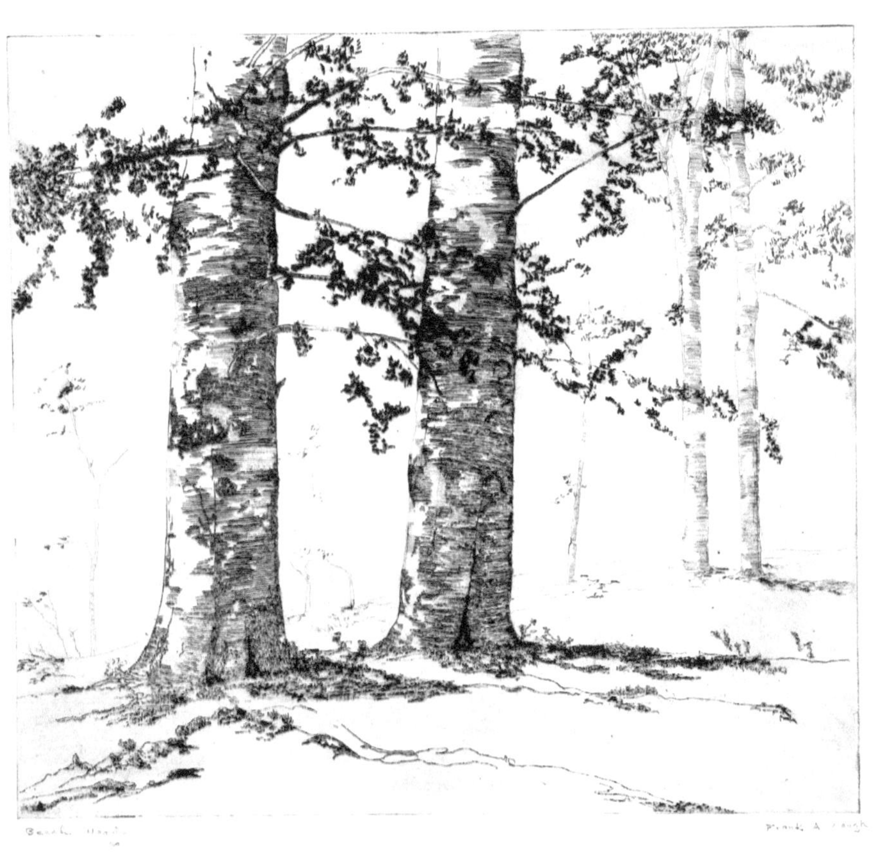

28. Beech Woods, 9x10, etching, Nov. 1939

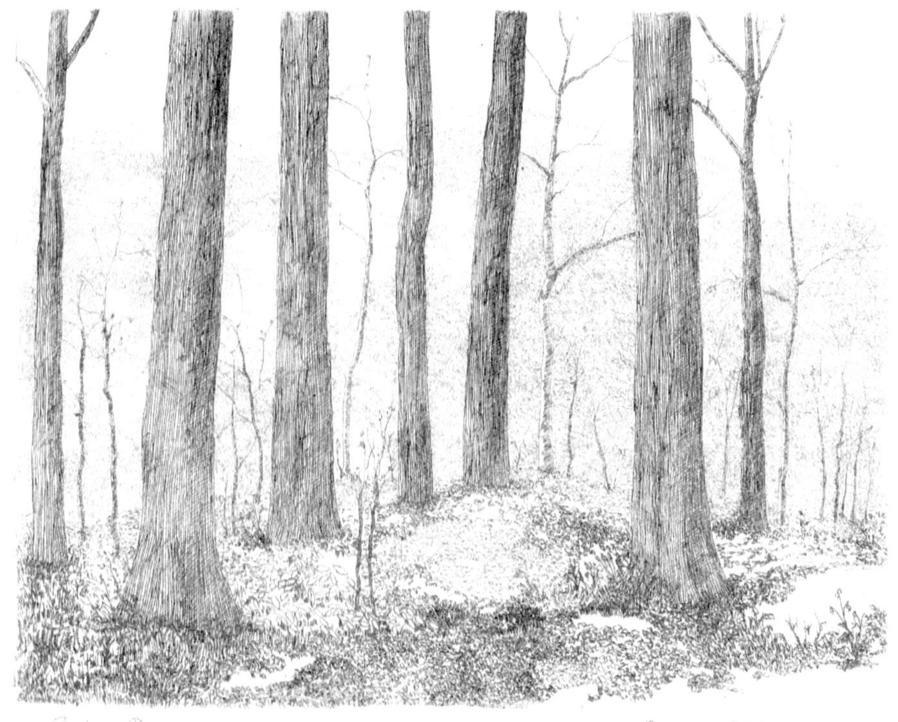

29. Tulip Trees, 7x9, etching, Aug. 1942

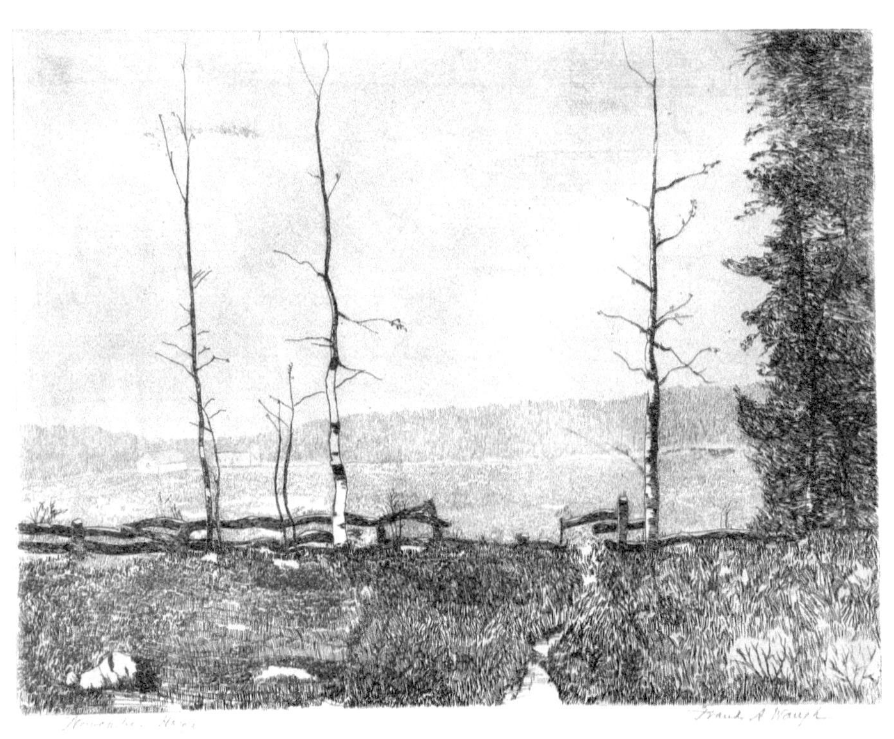

30. November Haze, 7x9, etching, Sep. 1942

Appendix

The List of Completed Etchings as Compiled by Waugh

FIRST SERIES

23. Old Mill - Williamsburg 5x5 1935

23a. Same, Second State

24. Dan Glazier's Mill – No. Leverett 5x7.................................1935 S*

25. The Gardener 5x5 1935

26. Early Days in California 5x7 ....1935 M*

27. Telegraph Hill - San Francisco 7x5 1935

28. Miami Palms 3x4 drypoint...1935

29. Roadside Maples 5x7 good..1935

30. Apple Tree in Winter 6x6 good..1935

31. Cape Cod Pines 7x5 drypoint-zinc..1935

32. White Willows in Winter 5x7 1935

33. Meiji Shrine - Tokyo 5x7 good...1936

34. Stockbridge House, MSC 5x7 good..1936

35. Covered Bridge at Lee 3x4 1936

36. Glimpse of East River, N. Y. 4x5 1936

37. Mexican Village 4x5 1936

38. Webster's Grist Mill-Northfield 5x4 good..............................1936 S*

39. Young Sycamores 8x6 1936

40. Quaker Meetinghouse 6x8..1936

40a. Same, Second State..1936

41. Flagg's Mill - Conway 5x7 1936

42. Sandhills - Kansas 5x7 drypoint zinc ....April 1936

43. Church on Florida Hill 4x5...April 1936

44. Mountain Cabin - N. C. 6x8 good ....April 1936

45. Leucojum 4x3, good ....May 1936

46. Kansas Barnyard 4x6 ....May 1936

47. Bee Skeps 4x5 ....May 1936

48. Theron Pratt's Mill, Jabish Brook, 5x7 ....June 1936

49. Oaks and Rocks, Ambleside, 4x5.....................................Sept 1936

50. Stonehenge 5x7 ....Sept 1936

SECOND SERIES

No. 51-Pollard Oaks, Epping Forest 6x6 ....Sept 1936 S*

No. 52-Mountain Cabin No. Carolina second state 6x8 .... Sept 1936

No. 53-Burnham Beeches 8x6 .... Oct 1936 S*

No. 54-Scotch Firs at Coniston, drypoint on zinc 7x5 .... Nov 1936

No. 55-Pelter Bridge, Ambleside 5x7 .... Nov 1936

No. 56-Cumberland Farm (England) 5x7 .... Nov 36 S*

No. 57-Ullswater 5x7 .... Dec 1936 S*

No. 58-Dudleyville Mill 5x7 .... Dec 1936 S*

No. 59-Worthington Mill 4x5 .... Dec 1936

No. 60—Sanctuary's Mill-Mill Valley 4x8 .... Dec 1936 S*

No. 61-Pouter Pigeon 5x4 .... Dec 1936

No. 62-Chestnut Boles 6x8 .... Dec 1936

No. 63-Cottonwoods, Virgin River, Utah 5x7 .... Jan 1937

No. 64-Bridge at Durham 6x8 .... Feb 1937 S*

No. 65-Pine Woods in Winter, Sunderland 7x7 .... Feb 1937 S*

No. 66-Gray Birches 6x6 .... Feb 1937

No. 67-Sugar Woods, Sunderland 5x7 .... Mar 1937 S*

No. 68-Mission Santa Barbara 8x4 .... Mar 1937

No. 69-Foot Hills 2x6 .... Mar 1937 S*

No. 70-Sugar Maples, Sunderland 7x9 .... Mar 1937

No. 71-Scrub Oak and. Dunes (drypoint) 7x5 .... Apr 1937 S*

No. 72-Abandoned Mill-Belchertown 5x7 .... Apr 1937 S*

No. 73-Tupelos, Fisher's Island 8x6 .... Apr 1937 S*

(note the chronology here: Waugh studied at the Fontainebleau School of Fine Arts in France, July and August, 1937; this may account for a disruption in numbers)

No. 74-Puffer's Mill, No. Amherst 5x7 .... Sept.1937 S*

No. 75-Old Cider Mill 5x7 .... Sept. 1937 S*

No. 76-Les Pins, Fontainebleau, (Pines at Fontainebleau)

5x4 .... July 1937

No. 77-Les *Hêtres*, Forêt de Fontainebleau 6x4 .... July 1937 M*

No. 78 Maison Millet, Barbison 4x5 .... July 1937 S, M*

No. 79 Le Jardin, Fontainebleau 5x7 .... Aug 1937 S*

No. 80 Lac aux Carps, Fontainebleau 4½ x7½ .... Aug 1937 S*, M*

No. 81 Fletcher's Grist Mill, Southwick 5x7 ....Oct. 1937 S*

No. 82 California Farm (California ranch)

5x8 (4 ¾ x8)..Oct 1937 M*

No. 83 Guilford's Mill, Ashfield 5x7 ....Oct 1937 S*

No. 84 Aspens at Crystal Lake 9x7..........................Oct 1937

No. 85 Fitts' Mill5x7................................Nov 1937 S*, M* (1935)

No. 86 Mill at North Amherst 5x8.........................Nov 1937 S*

No. 87 New London Tenements 4x5.......................Nov 1937 S*

No. 88 Fiske's Mill, Montague 3 ½ x6......................Nov 1937 S*

No. 89-Old Apple Tree 9x7..................................Dec 1937 S*

No. 90-Meadow Elm 6x6....................................Dec 1937

No. 91-Bowen's Mill 7x5.....................................Jan 1938 S*

No. 92-Roadside Elm 8x6....................................Jan 1938 S*

No. 93-Zoned for Manufacturing 5x8.....................Jan 1938 S*

No. 94-Bleak Winter 5x7.....................................Jan 1938

No. 95-Cotswold Corner 6x6...............................Jan 1938 S*

No. 96-Dan Glazier's Mill 5½ x8...........................Feb 1938

No. 97-Big Sycamore, Sunderland 7x5....................April 1938 S*

No. 98 Coronado Heights 3x5¾ ....April 1938 S*

No. 99 Hubbard's Sugarhouse 5x7 ....April 1938

No. 100 Old Plum Trees, Nara, Japan 7x5 ....May 1938 S*

THIRD SERIES

101. Mockernuts, Belchertown 5½ x8 ....May 1938 S*

102. Cryptomerias, Nara 8½x6..............................May 1938

103. Hubbard's Sugar House 5x7 ....June 1938

104. Joshua Tree, Mojave Desert 7x5.......................June 1938

105. Pines at Forest Lake, N.H. 5½ x8 ....July 1938

106. San Juan Capistrano 4x 6¼ ....July 1938

107. Healey's Sawmill, West Chesterfield 4x5 ....July 1938 S*

108. Sawmill, Cummington 4x5 ....July 1938 S*

109. Matsukaze no Matsu 5x7...............................Aug 1938 S*

110. Wethersfield Elm 6x6...................................Aug 1938 S*

111. Bradford's Mill, Williamsburg 3x6 .... Aug 1938 S*

112 Flagg's Mill, Conway 5x7 .... Aug 1938 S*

113. Watson's Mill, Moore's Corners 5x7 .... Aug 1938 S*

114. Gurley's Mill, Gurleyville, Conn. 5x7 .... Sept 1938 S*

115. The Learning Silo 3½x4½ .... Sept 1938 S*

116. Home Sweet Home 6x6 .... Sept 1938 S*

117. Willow by the Pool, 4x5 .... Nov 1938 S*

118. Agave (drypoint) 5x4 .... Dec 1938

119. Giant Oaks, Nara 9x7 .... Jan. 1939

120. Forest Rangers Cabin 6x6 .... Jan. 1939 S*

121. Live Oaks, California 5x7 .... Jan 1939

122. Red Pines, Bradford's Pond, N.H 5x7 .... Feb 1939 S*

123. Elms at Cambridge, Eng. 6x8 .... March 1939 S*, M*

124. Pasture Brook 4x7 .... March 1939 S*

125. Mill At Cushman 4x8 .... March 1939 S*

126. Hubbard's Sugar House 4½ x8 .... March 1939 M*

127. Bridge at Brattleboro 4x5 .... April 1939 S*

128. Mill at Southampton 4x5 .... April 1939 S*

129. Mill Pond at Moore's Corners 3x6 .... April 1939 S*

130. The Old Chapel 7x5 .... May 1939 S*

131. Oriental Planes (France) 8x6 .... June 1939 S*

132. Whipple's Mill, Bobbin Hollow 3x6 .... July 1939 S*

133. Grist Mill, Buckland 3x6 .... July 1939 S*

134. Maine Coast 3x6 .... Aug 1939 S(2)*

135. Farm in Maine 6x8 .... Aug 1939

136. Four Hickories 5x7 .... Aug 1939

137. Pitch, Cape Cod (Pitch Pine) 7x5 .... Sept. 1939 S(2)*, M* (1941)

138. Willows by the Bridge 6x6 .... Sept 1939 S*

139. Conway Bridge 4x8 .... Oct 1939 S*

140. Cottage in Volksberg 4x .... Oct 1939 S*

141. Beech Woods 9x10 .... Nov 1939 S*, M*

142. Willow Stump 7x5 .... Nov 1939 S*

143. Wash Day 7x7 .... Nov 1939 M(2)* (1937)

144. Fields of Hadley (dry point) 2½x4 ....Dec 1939 S*
145. Turbott's Creek 4x8 ....Dec. 1939
146. Meadow Brook 9x10 ....Jan. 1940 S*
147. Uncle Remus' Cabin 5x7 ....March 1940 S*
148. Key West 5x7 ....March 1940
149. House in Key West (Key West Architecture)
5x7 ....March 1940 M*
150. Cocoanut Palm 8½x6½ ....March 1940

FOURTH SERIES

151. Royal Palms 8x4 ....April, 1940 S*
152. Four Palmettoes 6½x8½ ....April 1940 S*, M*
153. Cypress Swamp 6½x8½ ....April, 1940 S*, M*
154. Live Oak 5x7 ....April 1940
155. Connecticut Stone Wall 5x8 ....May 1940 S*
156. Beech Trees & Rocks 5x7 ....June 1940 S*
157. Old Apple Orchard 5x8 ....June 1940
158. Sugar Tree 5x5 ....June 1940 S*
159. Soft Maple 4x5 ....July 1940
160. Horse Chestnut 7x5 ....July 1940
161. Fishing Village (Fisherman's Village) 5x7 ....July 1940 S*
162. Cottonwoods at Lake Champlain 5x7 ....July 1940 M*
163. Cedars and Birch 4x4 ....July 1940
164. White Oaks 5x8 ....July 1940 M*
165. Old Friends 5x7 ....Aug 1940
166. Pears 6x7½ ....Aug 1940
167. On the Beach 5x7 ....Aug 1940 S*
168. Spruce Swamp 3x6 ....Aug 1940 S*, M*
169. Ash Tree 6x8 ....Aug1940 S*
169b. Ibid 2nd state (Ash Tree) ....Dec. 1940 S(2)*, M*
170. Silvermine Bridge 5x4 ....Sept. 1940
171. Silvermine Bridge #2 3x6 ....Sept. 1940 S*, M*
172. Cape Cod 8x6 ....Oct 1940

173. Arbor Vitae 5¾ x 8 ½ ....Oct. 1940 S*

174. The Gate 8x8 ....Nov. 1940 M*

175. Roadside Pines, Cotuit 9x7 ....Nov. 1940 S*

176. Balsam Poplars (at Lake Champlain) 3½ x 4¾ .... Nov. 1940 M*

177. Little Waterfall 4x5 ....Dec. 1940 S*

178. On Mt. Toby (Sugar House) 4x5 ....Dec. 1940 M*

179. New Hampshire Elm 8x8 ....Dec. 1940 S*, M*

180. Camp Vassal 2x3 ....Dec. 1940 M*

181. Sugar House 8½ x12...Dec.1940

182. Gulf of Mexico 2x2 ....Jan 1941

183. The Big Oak 6x7¼ .... Jan. 1941 S*, M*

184. Slopes of Mt. Warner 6x7¼ ....Jan. 1941 S*

185. Study of a Sewer 8x6 ....Feb 1941 S*, M*

186. Young Arbor Vitaes 4x8 ....March 1941 M*

187. Cornfield 5x7 ....Feb- 1941 M*

188. Willows 2x3..March 1941 M*

189. Clam Digger 4x8 ....April 1941 S*, M*

190. Quiet Pool 4x8 ....April 1941 S*

191. Glazier's Mill (Saw Glazier's Mill) 2x3 ....May 1941 M*

192. Mt. Sugarloaf 2x3...May 1941

193. Barnyard Oak 8x8 ....June 1941 S*, M*

194. White Birches 5½ x8 ....June 1941 S*

195. Whale Inn 5x7 ....June 1941 S*

196 Monument to Wheat 6½ x8½ ....June 1941 S*

197. Grasshopper 5½ x8 ....July 1941

198. Mt. Holyoke 3x6...August 1941 S*

199. Mt. Toby 3x6 ....August 1941 S*

200. Passamaquoddy Bay 4x8 ....August 1941 S*

FIFTH SERIES

201. Elm of Many Stems 6x6...Sept 41 S*

202. Sugar House 8x12...Sept 41

203. Backwater 5x7...Mar 42 S*

204. Tiergarten Beeches 8½ x6½ ....Apr 42 S*
205. Woodbury's Sugar Woods 6½ x8½ ....May 42(2)*
206. Apple Tree in the Meadow 5x7 ....June 42 S*
207. Hemerocallis 6x3..June 42
208. Walnut Tree6x6...July 42 S*
209. Dogwoods - Early Spring 5x5...............................July 42 M*
210. David Grayson's Elm 8x8 ....July 42 S*
211. Douglas Fir 8x4..July 42 S*
212. Burnham Beeches 4x5..July 42 S*
213. Basswood 4x5 ....July 42 S*
214. Tulip Trees 7x9 ....Aug 42 S(2)*
215. November Haze 7x9..Sept 42 S*
216. Rendezvous 5x5 ....Oct 42 S*
217. Plymouth Rock 7x5 ....Nov 42 S*
218. Moon Bridge 5x7...Dec 42 S*
219. Pointers (Lombardy Poplar) 5x5 ....Dec 42 M*
220. Red Alder 7x5...Jan 43 S*
221. Magnolia 7x5...Jan 43
222. Honey Locust 7x5...Jan 43
223. Willows (2 old trees) 7x5...Feb 43 M*

*M denotes University Museum of Contemporary Art collection at UMass Amherst; these etchings are available to the public digitally.

*S denotes the Robert S. Cox Special Collections and University Archives Research Center, DuBois Library at UMass Amherst

A few etchings can also be found in the archives at the Tides Institute and Museum of Art in Eastport, ME, and the Mead Art Museum at Amherst College. Other etchings are in private collections.

Dimensions in inches, vertical given first.

Acknowledgments

To my friends, colleagues, students, and family, I could not have finished this book without your support. Especially for those who are no longer with us, I wish I had been able to finish the book earlier. I want to give special thanks to the following individuals: For arranging access in 1922 to the Frank A. Waugh Diaries Collection, 1923-1943, Ines Zalduendo, special collections archivist, at the Frances Loeb Library, Harvard University Graduate School of Design. For access to the Albert E. Waugh Papers, Betsy Pittman, University of Connecticut, then interim director and University Archivist, Thomas J. Dodd Research Center. For help locating all the Waugh and Woodbury possible connections, Sarah Hartwell, reading room supervisor, Rauner Special Collections Library: Archives, Manuscripts, Rare Books, Dartmouth College Library. At Kansas State University, Stephanie A. Rolley, professor and head, Department of Landscape Architecture/Regional and Community Planning; Maxine Ganske, library assistant, Weigel Library; and Anthony R. Crawford, CA, associate professor, university archivist/curator of manuscripts, Morse Department of Special Collections, Hale Library. Gratitude for support and a special tea event to Tevis Kimball, former head of special collections at The Jones Library, Amherst, Massachusetts. For careful review of my citations and permission to use them, Katherine Whitcomb, head of special collections at the Jones Library. For arrangements to access the Waugh collection gratitude to Robert S. Cox, former head, and Danielle Kovacs, head. Robert S. Cox Special Collections and University Archives Research Center, UMass Amherst Libraries. To Linda Flint McClelland for her entry on Waugh in the *Pioneers of American Landscape Design* (2000) and her extensive introduction to the 2007 reprint edition of Waugh's *Book of Landscape Gardening*. Tessa Veazey and Margaret Zoller, reference services, Smithsonian Archives of American Art for access to the George Pearse Ennis and Charles H. Woodbury materials. To Hugh French, director of the Tides Institute & Museum of Art, for his insights about the cultural legacy of printmaking in Maine. To Cori Sherman North, Curator at the Birger Sandzén Memorial Gallery for her help with archival records there. To Betsy Siersma, the former director of the University Gallery at UMass for information about Waugh etching acquisitions. To Jennifer Lind, collection manager and registrar at the University Museum of Contemporary Art, for access to the Waugh materials.

To the following professor emeriti at UMass from different disciplines for their insightful editorial review and comments on select chapters: Dr. John R. Mullin (regional planning); Dr. John Ahern (landscape architecture); Dr. Lyn Frazier (linguistics); and Dr. Richard Bogartz (psychology). To Professor Patricia McGirr for our Waugh memorial design studio at UMass. To Dr. Julius Gy. Fabos for sharing his approval and pride after reading the first draft. To Robert E. Grese, professor emeritus of environment and sustainability, University of Michigan, for his very helpful review of the manuscript. To historian and author, Ruth Owens Jones, for her help with Amherst history. For invaluable collegial support and advice from two former presidents of the Council of Educators in Landscape Architecture Dr. Alf Simon, professor emeritus, Department of Landscape Architecture, School of Architecture and Planning, University of New Mexico, and Kenneth R. Brooks, professor emeritus of landscape architecture, The Design School, Arizona State University. I want to remember my first etching and drawing teachers, Walter S. Feldman and Edward Koren, at Brown University for all their guidance. To Peter, Chris, and Judith Woodbury for their generous help with Charles H. Woodbury materials; Marcia Beal Brazer for a tour of the original Woodbury home and studio; and Carole Lee Carroll, museum curator, Ogunquit Heritage Museum, especially for her help with the Woodbury native tree drawings published by Milton Bradley. My appreciation to artist Alexandra Heintzelman Sharma for very helpful information about her grandfather, Arthur Heintzelman. Thanks to my photographer Ben Barnhart. All photographs of the etchings and drawings in the book unless otherwise noted are his able work.

To all the Waugh family members for their gracious sharing of family memories and records, especially Alice Collier Waugh, Dr. John S. and Susan Waugh, Prudence (Waugh) Donovan, Alfred W. Gillette, and Margaret Alice (Waugh) Maxfield. To my colleague Mark Resnick for sharing the passion of Waugh family research leading to his book *Dorothy Waugh: Unsung Master of Design, Renaissance Woman* (in production as of this date) and exhibit at the Poster House in New York scheduled for 2025-2026. To my son, Oliver (Marston), for his support of all things electronic especially for the early stages of this research. And to my husband, Chuck (Dr. Charles E. Clifton, Jr.), for being there to help throughout the past twelve years at every turn.

Endnotes

1   Steiner, Frederick R., and Kenneth R. Brooks. "Agricultural Education and Landscape Architecture." *Landscape Journal* 5, no. 1 (1986): 19-32.

2   From correspondence from Esther Gillette to graduate student James Mingus July 27, 1966 sent in response to his letter asking for information about Waugh for his proposed graduate thesis, now in possession of author.

3   Frank A. Waugh, "Some Notes on Timber-culture," *Garden and Forest* 8 (18 December 1895): 502–3; "Trees of Minor Importance for Western planting—I," G&F 9 (15 January 1896): 23; and "II," G&F 9 (29 January 1896): 42–43.

4   From entries August 31, and September 8, 1898 in personal journal, "Cornell Journal "(handwritten), loaned to the author by the great granddaughter Alice Collier Waugh and grandson, the late Dr. John Waugh, the brilliant M.I.T. Arthur Amos Noyes professor of chemistry and expert on nuclear magnetic resonance, (used with permission).

5   The grandson Dr. John Waugh described this to the author during visits to his home in April of 2010 in Lincoln, MA.

6   FAW, *Textbook of Landscape Gardening, Designed Especially for the Use of Non-professional Students*, New York: John Wiley & Sons, Inc., 1922:v

7   From an Oct 3, 1898 entry in the "Cornell Journal."

8   FAW, *Landscape Gardening*, Orange Judd, New York, 1899, p. 6.

9   FAW, Systematic Pomology, New York: Orange Judd, 1903: 6.

10   From the Oct 3, 1898 entry in the "Cornell Journal" see above endnote

11   [Robert Lane Wells, pseud]. "Alderbrook Farm, In Our Second Month of Country-Life-for-Profit, We Build a Chicken House and Do Some Practical Forestry," *Women's Home Companion* 42 (March 1915): 26.

12   [Robert Lane Wells, pseud]. "Alderbrook Farm in July, We do our haying in the old-fashioned way, We sow three kinds of cover crop, And we enjoy life," *Women's Home Companion* 42 (April 1915): 21.

13   [Robert Lane Wells, pseud], "Alderbrook Farm in July, We do our haying in the old-fashioned way, We sow three kinds of cover crop, And we enjoy life," *Women's Home Companion* 42 (July 1915): 18.

14 Letter from Frederick V. Waugh Gillette to James Mingus, July 30, 1966, sent in response to his letter asking for information about Waugh for a proposed graduate thesis project, in possession of author.

15 Rand, Frank Prentice, and Dan Frank Waugh. *Crumpled Leaves From Old Japan*. Amherst: [s.n.], 1922.

16 This author has a copy: Waugh, Dan Frank. *Matsukaze, a Japanese No Play by Kwanami*, New York: [s.n.], 1933.

17 For his papers, see "The Albert E. Waugh Papers," Archives and Special Collections, the Thomas J. Dodd Research Center, the University of Connecticut, Storrs: https://archives.lib.uconn.edu/islandora/object/20002%3A860133439

18 *Waugh, Albert E.* Sundials: Their Theory and Construction. *New York: Dover Publications, 1973.*

19 Houck, James P. and Martin E. Abel, editors. *Selected Writings on Agricultural Policy and Economic Analysis: Frederick V. Waugh*. Minneapolis, MN: University of Minnesota Press, 1984

20 The first book received some negative critical reviews-Waugh, Dorothy. *Emily Dickinson's Beloved*, a surmise, New York: Vantage Press, 1976; the second book was done six years before Dorothy passed. Waugh, Dorothy. *Emily Dickinson Briefly*. New York: Vantage Press, 1990.

21 For an excellent biography and account of Sidney's war contributions, see the Amherst College newsletter article at "Sidney Waugh, Monuments Man," by Pamela Russell and Sheila Flaherty-Jones, February 7, 2014, https://www.thecommononline.org/sidney-waugh-monuments-man/

22 "Atlantica," Corning Museum Facebook page. https://www.facebook.com/corningmuseumofglass/photos/a.93266165728/10157018517785729/?type=1&theater

23 Andrew W. Mellon Memorial Fact Sheet, https://www.nga.gov/content/dam/ngaweb/press/assets/2016/fountain/mellon-fountain-fact-sheet.pdf

24 For a detailed discussion of these contributions that are beyond the scope of this book, see McClelland, Linda Flint, Introduction to this edition, Waugh, Frank Albert *Book of Landscape Gardening*. United States: University of Massachusetts Press and Library of American Landscape History, 2007.

25 Last page of the F.A.W. Daily Diary, 1907, loaned by Dr. John Waugh and Alice Collier Waugh, and used with permission.

26 From a *History of the Department of Landscape Architecture & Regional Planning University of Massachusetts at Amherst* report for the purpose graduate program accreditation, 1970.

27 Jensen, Jens. 1939. *Siftings*. R. F. Seymour. https://search.ebscohost.com/login.aspx?direct=true&AuthType=ip,sso&db=cat09207a&AN=umf.oai.edge.fivecolleges.folio.ebsco.com.fs00001006.2bed484b.2e5b.5ec0.b7c0.8074b1395e4c&site=eds-live&scope=site.

28 Whether Waugh continued his friendship with Lange during the Nazi era is not known. With Waugh's sons military roles in the wars, he did not express any loyalty to Germany.

29 From a December 16, 1910 entry to Waugh's personal diary. The book mentioned is Lange, Willy and Otto Stahn, *Gartengestaltung der Neuzeit*, Verlag: Leipzig: Verlagsbuchhandlung von J. J. Weber, 1909.

30 From a December 16, 1910 diary entry; surviving diaries loaned to the author from the personal collection of the Waugh family.

31 Review, by Frank A. Waugh, Gartenbilder, *Landscape Architecture* Magazine, v.13, No.2 (April, 1923), p.218.

32 Ibid

33 *The Landscape Beautiful*, p.35.

34 Ibid, p36-37.

35 Waugh, Frank. *Landscape Beautiful*. Orange Judd. New York, 1912, pp.36-37.

36 Ibid, p.34.

37 Ibid, p.37.

38 Unsigned book review. *American Photography*, v.4, January 1, 1910, p. 300.

39 For a detailed discussion about use of the terms "Landscape Gardening" vs. "Landscape Architecture," see Steiner, Frederick R., and Kenneth R. Brooks. "Agricultural Education and Landscape Architecture." *Landscape Journal*, vol. 5, no. 1, 1986, pp. 19–32.

40 *Landscape Architecture Quarterly*,v.1, (October,1910) p.100. Hereafter abbreviated *LAQ*

41 A.S.L.A. Notes, *LAQ*, v. 14, No. 4 (July,1924), p.294.

42 *LAQ*, v.30, No.2 (Jan 1920), p.110.

43 *LAQ*, v1, (October 1910), p.100.

44 Schneider, Camillo K. *Landschaftliche gartengestaltung: insbesondere über die künstlerische verwertung natürlicher vegetationsvorbilder in den werken der gartenkunst und mit einem beitrag über heimatschutz und landesverschönerung.* Leipzig: C. Scholtze (W. Junghans), 1907.

45 *Landscape Architecture* 8, no. 2 (1918): 102.

46 Ibid: 103.

47 Orange Judd Publishing Company, Inc., New York, Kegan Paul, Trench, Trubner & Co., Ltd., 1930.

48   From the 1973 Master's Thesis by Joseph DiCarlo, Jr. chaired by Dr. Ervin H. Zube, LARP, UMass. Amherst.

49   Waugh, Frank. *Textbook of Landscape Gardening*. 1922. Orange Judd. New York, p.7.

50   Ibid, p.8.

51   Ibid, p. 10.

52   Waugh, Frank. *The Landscape Beautiful*. 1910. Orange Judd. New York, pp314-315.

53   Ibid. pp.318-319.

54   Waugh, Frank. "Art for All" *School and Society* 15, no. 382 (22 April 1922): 438.

55   *The Natural Style in Landscape Gardening*. Boston: Richard G. Badger, 1917: 93.

56   Ibid: 93.

57   Ibid: 94-95.

58   Ibid: 101.

59   Ibid: 51.

60   Landscape Engineering in the National Forests. Washington, D.C.: U.S. Department of Agriculture, Forest Service, 1918. And also see: *A Plan for the Development of the Village of Grand Canyon, Arizona*. Washington, D.C.: U.S. Department of Agriculture, Forest Service, 1918.

61   Unsigned, "Book Reviews." LA 9, no.1 (October 1918): 37-38.

62   "Large Scale Planning: The Mount Hood National Forest." *American Landscape Architect* 2, no. 6 (June 1930): 20–23.

63   "Landscape Conservation: Planning for the Restoration, Conservation, and Utilization of Wilds Lands for Park and Forest Recreation." Manuscript, August 1935. U.S. Department of the Interior, National Park Service.

64   Marie Luise Gothein, *Geschichte der Gartenkunst. Band 1: Von Ägypten bis zur Renaissance in Italien, Spanien und Portugal. Band 2: Von der Renaissance in Frankreich bis zur Gegenwart*. Herausgegeben mit Unterstützung der Königlichen Akademie des Bauwesens in Berlin. (Berlin: Diederichs, 1914, 1926)

65   "Landscape Architecture in North America, United States and Canada: Historical and Critical Survey," in *A History of Garden Art*, ed. Marie Luise Gothein, 3rd ed. (New York: Dutton, 1928):424.

66   "Water Running Down Hill." *American Forests and Forestry Life* 31 (June 1925): 352–53.

67   "Running Water." *LA* 22, no. 4 (July 1932): 270–80.

68   "The Physiography of Ponds and Lakes." LA 22, no. 2 (January 1932): 89-99.

69 "Natural Plant Groups, *LA* 21, no. 3 (April 1931): 169-179.

70 November 15, 1921 Daily Diary entry, courtesy of the Waugh family.

71 https://sites.google.com/site/tinshopmuseumshubenacadiens/history-of-shubenacadie-ns

72 Letter from Ray Stannard Baker (RSB) to Frank A. Waugh (FAW), June 12, 1942. Ray Stannard Baker Collection (Series 2B: Correspondence from Frank & Dorothy Waugh), Special Collections, The Jones Library, Amherst, Mass. Hereafter abbreviated SC TJL.

73 "Joys of Fishless Fishing in Streams and Elsewhere." Countryside 19 (October 1914): 185.

74 Letter from RSB to FAW, June 12, 1942. RSB Collection (Series 2B), SC TJL.

75 Letter from RSB to FAW, October 16, 1942. RSB Collection (Series 2B), SC TJL

76 "Maine Art Schools and Museums," Maine Library Bulletin, Volume XIII, January 1928, No. 3, p.71

77 *Ennis, George Pearse, 1933. Making a Water-colour. How to Do It Series. London: Studio Publications. No. 3.*

78 American Art Annual, volume 20, 1923, p 225

79 "Valuable Art Exhibit Shown in Mem Building, Colorful Ocean Scenes by G.P. Ennis Now Being Shown in Memorial Hall," Massachusetts Collegian, November 18, 1931, p.1.

80 "Fine Paintings on Exhibition, Works of George Pearse Ennis Are Secured by Professor Waugh" Massachusetts Collegian, January 8. 1930, pp.1, 3.

81 West, Levon, 1932. *Making an Etching. How to Do It Series. London: Studio Publications. No. 1.*

82 Sometimes etching may be used as a general umbrella term to refer to an intaglio print without much distinction, whether it is from hardground or drypoint, or from other methods such as those of softground or aquatint.

83 According to printmaking Professor Walter Feldman from Brown University, 1970, and artist Reinhard Wiedemer, Freiburg, Germany 2003.

84 Per phone communication with granddaughter Margaret Waugh Maxfield, 3.17.2010 and meeting with granddaughter Prudence Waugh 10.9.2003.

85 "Interesting Exhibit By Prominent Artists in Mem. Building, Watercolor Paintings and Lithographs—Works of George Ennis and Robert Craig," Massachusetts Collegian, December 12, 1935. pp. 1, 6.

86 Wiley & Sons, New York.

87 Letter home from Sidney Waugh, January 30[1927]. Waugh Family Collection (Series 3D), SC TJL.

88 Winlock, H.E., Metropolitan Museum of Art Bulletin, v. 31, No. 10, p. 197

89   Waugh, Dorothy. *Among the Leaves and Grasses*, Henry Holt, NY, 1931.

90   Letter from Sidney Waugh to Dorothy Waugh, undated. Waugh Family Collection (Series 4C: Correspondence with Waugh, Sidney) SC TJL.

91   Dodd, Mead, and Company, NY, 1938.

92   Waugh, Frank A., Kansas State College, Class of 1891, Class Letter, Fifty Years After, 1941. Special Collections Library, Kansas State University, Manhattan, KS, 36 pages (LD2668 .A7 1891b).

93   Letter from FAW to DW, undated, SC TJL. Although undated, the time of the writing can be narrowed down between June and July of 1939 from other details in the letter.

94   Art Colony Walking Tour, Ogunquit Museum of American Art, ogunquitmuseum.org.

95   Woodbury, Charles Herbert. *Painting and the Personal Equation*. Boston and New York: Houghton Mifflin Company, 1919.

96   I am grateful to Carole Lee Carroll, Museum Curator of the Ogunquit Heritage Museum, who shared copies of these. See Woodbury, Charles H. (Charles Herbert), 1864-1940. *Pencil Sketches of Native Trees*. Springfield, Mass.: Milton Bradley Co., 1905.

97   Woodbury Family, Black Book, Book 4, Plate 1 66Af.

98   For more justice to Woodbury's greatness beyond the relevance to the focus here on Waugh, see Loria, Joan and Warren A. Seamans. *Earth, Sea and Sky*, Charles H. Woodbury. Cambridge, MA: MIT Museum of MIT, 1988.

99   Drawing Trees, *American Forest*. (November 1942): 499-501.

100   As per a note attached to the etching in the author's collection.

101   Smith, Donald Eugene. The Prints of Arthur Wm. Heintzelman. Boston: Boston Public Library, 2004.

102   Educator's Hobby Is Experimenting With Photographs. *The Christian Science Monitor* (April 4) 1922: F1.

103   Culver, Michael. *Charles Woodbury and His Students*, Ogunquit Museum of American Art, July 1-August 12, 1998, Ogunquit, ME: Ogunquit Museum of American Art, 1998.

104   In 1944 the executors of Woodbury's estate, Mrs. Charles Bruen Perkins and Mr. and Mrs. David O. Woodbury, the artist's son and daughter-in-law, donated a complete set of prints, including a number of trial proofs and etching plates, and also drawings, watercolors, and oil paintings to the Boston Public Library's collection of works by Woodbury. There are 1,550 prints, 486 drawings, 86 watercolors, 51 oil paintings, and 38 copper plates; the prints and related drawings have been digitized. https://www.digitalcommonwealth.org/

collections/commonwealth:9s161k40g.

105 From the September 30, 1940 entry, *FAWDC*.

106 For detailed information about the Dorothy Waugh's employment with the National Park Service archives, consult- National Park Service archive, Record Group no.: 79 Records of the National Park Service. Stack Area: 150. Row: 35. Compartment: 9. Shelf: 6. Box: 41 (Entry: P 90. State Park Files, 1933-1947.) and https://www.archives.gov/research/guide-fed-records/groups/079.html

107 "Waugh Discusses New Art Exhibit in Mem. Building," *Massachusetts Collegian*, October 26, 1936:1

108 "Prof. F.A. Waugh to Talk on Etchings at Amherst College," *The Amherst Record*, January 18, 1937:1. Hereafter abbreviated AR.

109 "Exhibition of Prints At Jones Library," *AR*, October 14, 1936:1.

110 *AR*, January 12, 1938: 1.

111 The President's Report for 1940-1941. Ann Arbor, University of Michigan. 43 no.2 (December 1941):120.

112 The Art Registrar Birger Sandzén Memorial Gallery in Lindsborg, KS (October 7) 1936.

113 The Art Registrar Birger Sandzén Memorial Gallery in Lindsborg, KS (February 18) 1937: 12-13.

114 FAW "Studies from the Nude." *Country Life and the Sportsman* 75 (December 1938): 60–62.

115 FAW. "A Fading Remnant, Etchings of Old Sawmills," *Survey Graphic* 28, 1939:434-35.

116 *American Forests* (November) 1942: 499. Hereafter abbreviated *AF*.

117 *AF*: 510

118 Letter from Frank A. Waugh (FAW) to Dorothy Waugh (DW), dated "Sunday Afternoon".The Waugh Family Collection (WFC), Series 4C: Correspondence with Waugh, Frank, SC TJL.{The completed etching referenced is listed with a May 1942 date on FAW's list; this letter may be from May 31, 1942.}

119 Letter from FAW to DW, dated "Sunday Morning". WFC (Series 4C), SC TJL.

120 Letter from FAW to DW, dated "Tuesday Forenoon". WFC (Series 4C), SC TJL.

121 Letter from FAW to DW, dated "Tuesday noon". WFC (Series 4C), SC TJL.

122 Letter from FAW to DW, dated "Saturday night". WFC (Series 4C), SC TJL. {Among FAW's list of etchings, there is a "November Haze" etching from September 1942 which suggests the date may be close to then}.

123 Email from Margaret Alice Waugh Maxfield to author, March 10, 2010.

9 798888 243343